# START YOUR OWN
# PHOTOGRAPHY
# BUSINESS

# Additional titles in **Entrepreneur's Startup Series**

## **Start Your Own**

# Entrepreneur
## MAGAZINE'S

 **STARTUP**

# START YOUR OWN
# PHOTOGRAPHY
# BUSINESS

### Third Edition

## YOUR STEP-BY-STEP GUIDE
## TO SUCCESS

The Staff of Entrepreneur Media, Inc. & Jason R. Rich

Entrepreneur Press®

Publisher: Entrepreneur Press
Cover Design: Andrew Welyczko
Production and Composition: Eliot House Productions

© 2019 by Entrepreneur Media, Inc.
All rights reserved.
Reproduction or translation of any part of this work beyond that permitted by Section 107 or 108 of
the 1976 United States Copyright Act without permission of the copyright owner is unlawful. Requests
for permission or further information should be addressed Entrepreneur Media Inc. Attn: Legal
Department, 18061 Fitch, Irvine, CA 92614.

This publication is designed to provide accurate and authoritative information in regard to the subject
matter covered. It is sold with the understanding that the publisher is not engaged in rendering legal,
accounting, or other professional services. If legal advice or other expert assistance is required, the
services of a competent professional person should be sought.

Entrepreneur Press° is a registered trademark of Entrepreneur Media, Inc.

**Library of Congress Cataloging-in-Publication Data**
Names: Rich, Jason, editor. | Entrepreneur Press. | Entrepreneur Media, Inc., issuer.
Title: Start your own photography business / by The Staff of Entrepreneur Media, Inc. and
    Jason R. Rich.
Description: Third edition. | Irvine, California : Entrepreneur Press, [2019] | Series: Startup |
    Includes index.
Identifiers: LCCN 2019019962| ISBN 978-1-59918-657-3 (alk. paper) | ISBN 1-59918-657-8
    (alk. paper)
Subjects:  LCSH: Photography--Business methods.
Classification: LCC TR581 .E58 2019 | DDC 770.68--dc23
LC record available at https://lccn.loc.gov/2019019962

Printed in the United States of America

23  22  21  20  19                                                                 10 9 8 7 6 5 4 3 2 1

# Contents

## Chapter 7
# Business Structure: A Blueprint for Success ........ 69

## Chapter 8
# Business Equipment for the Photographer ........... 83

## Chapter 9
# Help Wanted: Staffing Your Studio ................. 93

## Chapter 10
# Marketing Made Easy ........................ 101

**Chapter 14**

## More Expert Advice from Experienced Pros . . . . . . . . . .149

**Appendix**

## Resources . . . . . . . . . . . . . . . . . . . . . . . . . . . . . . . . . . . . .175

## Glossary . . . . . . . . . . . . . . . . . . . . . . . . . . . . . . . . . . . . .179

## Index . . . . . . . . . . . . . . . . . . . . . . . . . . . . . . . . . . . . . . . .181

# Preface

In some respects, transforming your passion as an amateur photographer into a lucrative career as a professional photographer has never been easier. High-end digital cameras are more powerful than ever, plus there are endless marketing and advertising possibilities available on the internet that make it easier to showcase your work and potentially attract paying customers or clients.

The moment you decide to take that leap from amateur or semiprofessional photographer to professional photographer, however, you'll immediately be taking on a wide range of additional responsibilities that go well beyond tapping your creative talents so you can consistently take eye-catching and emotion-provoking photos.

For many, becoming a professional photographer means operating a legal business entity as an entrepreneur and small-business owner. This requires you to handle many business-related tasks, such as sales, bookkeeping/accounting, advertising, marketing, and customer relations.

For example, you'll need to set up and maintain an office, gallery, and/or photo studio, and make sure you have the proper insurance based on the type of work you're doing. As a photographer, you'll also need to take, edit, print, organize, and sell your photographs, and manage that complete work flow, while maintaining your photography equipment and related gear.

Plus, in today's world, it's essential for photographers to create and maintain a professional-looking web presence with a website and online portfolio to showcase their work. You'll likely find it necessary to become professionally active on social media (Facebook, Instagram, Twitter, Pinterest, and LinkedIn, for example), to find and interact with potential clients, and for marketing and showcasing your work online.

It will also be necessary to ramp up your level of technical expertise. Today's professional-level digital cameras and accessories are complex, and you'll need to become a pro when it comes to understanding and using your equipment. In addition, once images are shot, they need to be transferred to a computer to be managed, edited, organized, printed, shared, and archived, for example. Some of these tasks typically require the utilization of a secure cloud-based service. In other words, today's professional photography world is one that operates and thrives online.

The goal of this book is to help you identify and successfully handle the many tasks you'll be responsible for as a professional photographer. You'll discover that it's essential to establish your business with a strong foundation and with a well-defined set of goals. It's then your responsibility to operate your business in a smooth, efficient, sensible, and ethical way.

From this book, you'll discover there are many potential paths to follow once you choose to work as a professional photographer. In some cases, you'll be working for someone else. However, in many cases, you'll need to set up and maintain your own business, be your own boss, and establish your own work ethic. You'll be the one deciding when and where you work, what types of photographs you'll be taking, and who you'll be taking on as customers or clients. You'll also need to develop and fine tune your own photographic and artistic style to help your work stand out.

Moving forward, you'll need to make a lot of decisions and juggle many responsibilities (often simultaneously). Making the right decisions will likely lead to success and profits. Making the wrong decisions can easily lead to financial losses, legal liabilities, and the need to spend a lot of time and money correcting problems that arise but that could have easily been avoided.

The more business-related experience you have, the better equipped you'll be to make intelligent decisions when it comes to operating, growing, and legally protecting your new photography business. If you have zero business-related experience, you're not yet tech-savvy, and you're not comfortable using the internet, you're at a disadvantage—even if you're a highly skilled photographer.

The goal of this book is to help you understand what it will take to establish yourself as a professional photographer. You'll discover what types of opportunities exist and learn ways to take full advantage of your creative and artistic skills as a photographer.

It's important to understand that this book is for photographers, but it's not about the technical aspects of photography. From this book, you will not learn how to take or edit pictures, for example. Instead, this book is all about how to set up and run a photography business (from your home, an office, or a studio) and pursue what will hopefully become a lucrative career as a professional photographer. This is an easy-to-understand, information-filled, business-oriented, "how-to" book. It will provide you with the information you need to establish, maintain, and grow your photography business both online ad in the real world.

# Welcome to the Wonderful World of Photography

D igital photography is both a skill and an art form. This can also be said about being a business operator or an entrepreneur. On the digital photography side, the "skill" aspect means knowing how to operate your digital camera and related photography equipment. The "art form" part of digital photography requires you to constantly tap your creativity when it comes to choosing your subjects, framing your shots, and using the best available lighting to consistently take eye-catching, professional-looking, well-lit, thought-provoking, and artistic shots.

Operating a photography business also requires skill and creativity—just a different kind. There are many business-oriented skills you'll need to handle the day-to-day operation of your business. You'll also need to use your creativity to discover unique and innovative ways to find and generate customers, promote your business, and successfully deal with your competition.

But before most professional photographers reach that point, they typically begin as enthusiastic amateurs who discover they have a real talent for capturing creative images. Once they are bitten by the shutterbug, these hobbyists immerse themselves in the world of photography, while investing potentially thousands of dollars in equipment and related gear.

To help defray the costs, amateurs sometimes sell their images to stock companies or occasionally use their artistic talents to photograph weddings and other events. Some use their skills to provide more targeted or niche forms of photography, such as product or real estate photography, to local businesses. This is when a hobbyist starts the crossover into the world of professional photography—to help monetize this expensive hobby into a great side gig or a full-blown business.

Starting a part- or full-time career in photography is an excellent way to blend a passion with a steady income. Photographers can turn a fun hobby into a lucrative business that

## ▶ Professional Photographers Have a Lot of Competition

Looking back just three to five years, professional photographers used high-end cameras and were experts at using them. Today, everyday people can capture professional-quality images using the cameras built into their smartphones. In fact, more than 1.3 trillion photos are taken using smartphones every year. As a result, there's less of a need to rely on professional photographers for many types of consumer photography needs.

For professional photographers to earn a successful living, not only do they need to use high-end camera equipment capable of shooting extremely high-resolution images, but it's also necessary to demonstrate that their work is vastly superior (in terms of artistic appeal and creativity) to what amateurs are capable of creating themselves. Becoming an expert at image editing as well as sales, marketing, and advertising (to find and land clients) is as important as having top-notch photography skills and the right equipment.

can easily be operated from home or in a commercial location. Of course, there is a lot more to running a photography business (and working as a professional photographer) than just snapping pictures.

A photography business can be a full-time operation with employees or a part-time weekend venture that you can expand as desired. Beyond investing thousands of dollars to acquire the right photography equipment and gear, you'll need additional investment to acquire business-related equipment, tools, and resources, then properly brand and advertise, market, and promote your business both in the real world and online.

# Learning Where You Fit

In this guide, you'll discover useful tips for establishing your business and setting up a home office, traditional office, and/or studio, plus discover how to create and manage a professional-looking website and online-based portfolio to showcase and share your work.

You'll also learn how to use social media and online advertising, for example, to find and land new customers and clients. Depending on what type of photography you choose to specialize in, it might also be necessary for you to work with galleries or find other places (in the real world and/or online) where you can showcase and potentially sell your work.

You're about to discover that calling yourself a "professional photographer," or running a "photography business," can mean many things. There are many photography specialties you can focus on, which will appeal to specific types of customers or clients.

For example, you can specialize in:

▶ Commercial photography
▶ Corporate event photography
▶ Fashion photography
▶ Real estate photography
▶ Photojournalism (working for a newspaper, magazine, or news-oriented website)
▶ Product photography
▶ Portrait and headshot photography
▶ Travel photography
▶ Wedding photography and/or event photography (shooting parties, bar mitzvahs, and other occasions)
▶ Pet/animal photographer
▶ Fine art photographer (showcasing and selling your work through galleries and online to collectors and art connoisseurs)

Based on your skills, experience, interests, and camera equipment, this guide will help you determine which area(s) of photography you'll be good at, then help you identify money-making opportunities in that area.

## Learning to Monetize

Once you set yourself up running a photography business or working as a professional photographer, you'll need to set prices for your work. What you charge needs to be competitive but still allow you to earn a profit based on the amount of time, effort, and resources you use fulfilling the requirements of each assignment or job. Tips for setting your pricing, based on the services you provide, are also included in this guide. However, when it comes to setting your prices, the geographic region you work in, how much competition you have, and what experience and unique skills you bring to each assignment or job will all help you determine what your clients/customers will be willing and able to pay.

In some situations, it makes sense to charge an hourly rate. Other types of jobs will require you to charge a pre-negotiated half-day, full-day, or per-project rate. When it comes to selling or licensing images to a stock photo agency, advertising agency, or other business entity, for example, your client may pay a licensing fee for the right to use specific images or pay a flat fee to acquire the ownership and copyright of specific images.

Speaking of copyrights, permissions, and ownership of photography, as a professional photographer, you need to understand basic legal principles when taking photographs, including how to protect yourself from and prevent copyright infringement. You also need to know when it's necessary to obtain a signed release from your subject(s) and understand when and where you're legally able to take photos, especially at events or when on private property. Thus, basic legal, copyright, and business knowledge is required for most photography-related careers.

## Building Your Skill Set

Ultimately, you'll need to effectively combine your creative camera skills, photography equipment, and business know-how. Once you discover how to do this, you'll have the skill set to evolve from being a hobbyist into a professional photographer and business owner. One thing that makes photography such an attractive career choice is the ability to ease into it as quickly or as leisurely as you desire. This type of progression is one that few other occupations allow. With that being said, however, it's essential that you possess professional-level photography skills and training and have professional-quality equipment at your disposal before you're able to call yourself a "professional."

There are all sorts of ways to acquire photography training and learn how to take and edit photographs. You can go to school and study photography or gain real-world and hands-on experience apprenticing at an established photography studio. However, even with the best education under your belt, you'll still need at least some natural, artistic, and creative ability (that can't be taught). This is what can set your work apart from your competition. Sure, having the best camera and equipment on the market will help you, but being able to use that equipment to consistently capture visually appealing, professional-quality, unique, and creative images is what will make you marketable as a photographer.

Photographers are far more likely to work for themselves than people in most other occupations, according to the *Occupational Outlook Handbook,* published by the Department of Labor's Bureau of Labor Statistics. Overall, the bureau counted some 147,300 people in the country who held jobs as photographers in 2017. Of these, more than

## ▶ The World Has Gone Digital—So Should You!

If you've been interested in photography for a long time, you're probably accustomed to working with traditional, film-based cameras. In today's high-tech world, most professional photographers now rely on professional-level, digital SLR cameras and, most recently, on high-resolution, full-frame, mirrorless digital cameras (from companies like Nikon, Canon, Leica, Hasselblad, Sony, Olympus, Panasonic, or Fujifilm).

While there's still a small specialty market for photographers who shoot with film, especially in the fine art world, for most other types of photography, it's expected that you'll be using the latest in digital camera equipment.

Choosing the best digital camera gear based on your chosen specialty is one of the topics covered in Chapter 4, "The Digital Revolution." Since most professional photography work in the 21st century requires the use of a high-end digital camera, this is what's primarily covered within this guide.

Keep in mind, however, that even if you're using what was up until recently a cutting-edge digital SLR camera, thanks to recent technological advancements, it's likely time for you to upgrade to one of the latest full-frame, mirrorless digital cameras (with compatible lenses). This equipment upgrade will likely require you to make an additional equipment investment of $5,000 to $10,000 (although prices are likely to drop within a year or two, once this technology becomes more established).

half were self-employed, working in such specialty areas as portrait or wedding photography, advertising and product photography, and photojournalism. Photo studios doing portrait or commercial work, newspapers, magazines, advertising agencies, and online-based businesses/services made up most of the salaried positions.

Recent career-related research shows that the job market for professional photographers is facing challenges. In part, this is due to the introduction of more powerful, consumer-oriented cameras (and cameras built into smartphones) that have the ability to take professional-quality pictures with less technical know-how. That being said, what will allow you to achieve success as a pro photographer will ultimately be your creativity and your ability to differentiate your work from others by developing a unique style.

**tip**

Beyond knowing how to work your photography equipment, according to the *Occupational Outlook Handbook*, important skills and qualities needed to be a professional photographer include artistic ability, and business, customer service, and interpersonal skills. You also need to be detail- and deadline-oriented, and able to properly manage your time and problem-solve quickly.

## Learn from the Pros

Many people learn by doing to acquire the knowledge they need, when they need it. In many aspects of your life, that's fine. However, when it comes to becoming a business operator, there's little room to make mistakes. You're better off starting the business already possessing the skills, experience, and knowledge you'll need. This will help you overcome obstacles and challenges, and avoid costly and time-consuming mistakes.

As you read this book, one of your goals should be to avoid mistakes others have made and discover what works and what doesn't work in the real world when it comes to creating, managing, and growing your photography business. That's why this guide is chock full of exclusive and in-depth interviews with well-established and experienced photographers, as well as with representatives from companies that offer products or services to professional photographers.

You'll discover from these interviews that each photographer got into this career in a unique way, acquired their training differently, then used their core skill set and entrepreneurial spirit to transform their passion for photography into a lucrative career.

For example, you'll read about Michael Weschler, a bicoastal lifestyle, celebrity, and commercial photographer who was known as "the kid with the camera" when he was just

**tip**

Chapter 14 features in-depth, exclusive interviews with a handful of experienced and successful professional photographers who focus on a variety of different specialties. In these interviews, the featured photographers share their wisdom and advice, plus offer tips for avoiding common mistakes made by newcomers in the photography field.

seven years old. Weschler loved taking pictures, but it never occurred to him that he might be an artist. "When I was young, I always equated being an artist with going mad, like Van Gogh," he explains.

It wasn't until his junior year in college, while taking a photography class, that this architecture student discovered the magic that happens in a darkroom. "After breezing through the class, I started doing street photography and fine artwork on the side," explains Weschler.

"Then I switched my major to fine art and started taking classes for drawing, sculpture, painting, and all related disciplines." This was when he decided to pursue photography as a career. "Initially I thought I was going to be a gallery guy and do fine art photography," he says. "But I was really torn with the whole art-in-commerce dilemma and trying to find a balance."

Weschler explained that it wasn't until he started working with other photographers that he realized there was a place for him in commercial photography. He adds, "This was an area where I could create work for other people—as opposed to doing it for myself—and still feel like an artist." Today, Weschler is a renowned lifestyle and celebrity photographer whose works have been featured in *GQ*, *The New York Times*, *Allure*, *Food & Wine*, *In Style*, and many other publications. He works in both Los Angeles and New York City.

You'll also get to know Jerry Clement, who started his photography career before he could even drive. When he was just 12 years old, Clement shot his first wedding. "It wasn't anything elaborate, and all I had was an old Ansco box camera. But it was a great experience," he recalled. A few years later, he became the photographer for his high school yearbook. Upon graduation, he kept up his

**fun fact**

Today, women make up about half of all photographers, according to Professional Women Photographers (www.pwponline.org), an organization that formed in 1975 when some female photographers decided there was a need for women to band together to "support each other in the male-dominated photography arena." While women have corrected the imbalance, the group continues to offer networking, advocacy, and other resources.

## ► Part Time vs. Full Time

Many photographers—particularly homebased ones—start their business on a part-time basis, then gradually move into a full-time operation. This process allows for more flexibility, especially if you want to keep a steady cash flow coming while you establish your photography business. Also, if your current job offers a benefits package that includes insurance and retirement, that's another incentive to keep your homebased business as a part-time operation.

Starting part time gives you the opportunity to gain professional experience and build a solid reputation and portfolio as a photographer, while reducing some of the risk.

interest in the photography field as a hobby. However, it wasn't until 30 years later when Clement retired as an insurance auditor that he decided to pursue his vision of becoming a professional photographer specializing in fine art.

Before joining the digital generation, he mastered the rare technique of processing Ilfochrome prints (formally known as Cibachrome), which is still preferred by some art galleries and collectors because of its archival properties, not to mention its stunning color clarity. Today, Clement's fine art images are displayed in local galleries and grace the walls of residences and commercial offices of discerning art collectors.

Sometimes, success in the photography business happens later in life. Ray Strawbridge of Bunn, North Carolina, graduated from college in 1976 with a degree in broadcasting, journalism, and speech. He worked a few months as an audiovisual director before moving to his wife's hometown to help with the family grocery business. Shortly thereafter, he opened a small photography studio in a nearby college town to do portraitures and framing—with minimal success. "My wife reminded me after a couple of years that I wasn't getting rich," he chuckles. "So, I started doing contract photography work with the local community college system."

Strawbridge closed his studio and worked on-site at campus laboratories, which eventually segued into more lucrative assignments. It wasn't until he started working for a log cabin company that he found his niche. "That's when I really got into architectural photography," he recalls. "I traveled up and down the East Coast taking pictures of log cabin homes to be used in advertisements, planning guides, and magazine publications."

Since then, Strawbridge has produced thousands of images for magazine covers, feature stories, annual reports, and advertisements, specializing in architectural, product, industrial, and food photography, as well as executive portraiture.

Sometimes, success in the photography business happens when you least expect it. Alexi Killmer is a children's and family portrait photographer working on location in and around the Chicago area. She stumbled on her niche shortly after giving birth to her twin boys in 2004. "I immediately started photographing my boys and was told I should seriously consider doing this for others," recalls Killmer. It was a result of encouragement from family and friends that she decided to pursue a professional photography career.

In 2005, Killmer began taking on clients, and her business has been steady ever since. Today, she is a widely recognized child portrait photographer whose specialties include family lifestyle photography; in-home, on-location portrait sessions; and studio portrait sittings. Her favorite subjects are newborns, babies, children, maternity, and high school seniors.

These are just some of the photographers you'll be hearing from throughout this guide, each of whom shares their unique knowledge and advice, based on their own experiences and philosophies. Keep in mind, much of the advice you'll receive by reading these interviews applies to becoming a pro photographer, regardless of your chosen specialty. Thus, even if a photographer specializes in wedding, corporate, or fine art photography, and the specialty you plan to pursue is child or pet portrait photography, there's still a lot of useful information you can learn.

## Looking Ahead

Eugene Mopsik, executive director of the American Society of Media Photographers (ASMP), says, "There are two facets to photography: the creative side and the business side." Mopsik recommends that serious photographers learn everything they can about the day-to-day procedures and cost of doing business, including budgeting and insurance.

He explains, "You can be a great photographer, but if you have poor business acumen, you might be in business for a while, but you'll be losing money."

To help you find your balance, it's important to obtain an overview of the market, look at the specific services you'll want to consider offering, and then go through the step-by-step process of properly setting up your new venture.

In this book, you'll learn more about the basic requirements and startup costs, day-to-day operational expenses and considerations, and what to do when things don't go according to plan. Just as important, later chapters will focus on the sales, advertising, and marketing process, as well as how to track and manage the financial side of your business.

What you won't learn is how to get rich quick or become an overnight success. Being a professional photographer requires hard work, dedication, skill, an entrepreneurial spirit, creativity, and commitment. That's what running a business is about. You're going to love parts of the process, but you're responsible for all aspects of running your own business, so you can't skip steps or cut corners.

# Make Things Click by Finding Your Niche

There are many paths you can take that lead to a successful career working in photography. Once you've made the decision and commitment to enter this vast field, and before you can start the business planning process, you must first decide—at least tentatively—what type of photography you're interested in pursuing.

As you consider the niche you want to get into, think about your own likes and dislikes, skills, and resources. Take into account the time and financial commitment you're able to make, your personality, and the photography equipment you already own or have access to. For example, a photojournalist's job is to capture spontaneous moments in a wide range of settings with minimal equipment. On the other hand, a portrait photographer needs patience, must be willing to invest time to stage their shots, and must direct their subjects to achieve the perfect pose and facial expression.

This chapter focuses on just some of the popular photography specialties that professional photographers can pursue. And while the options are vast, it's important to keep in mind that thanks to evolving technologies and the changing media consumption habits of consumers, the demand for some specialties is diminishing.

After all, the prices for consumer-oriented point-and-shoot as well as digital SLR cameras have dropped, while their capabilities have increased. In addition, powerful cameras are now being built into the latest smartphones. As a result, even without a formal photography education or training, many amateur photographers are able to capture their own high-quality images and are no longer as inclined to hire a professional photographer.

Meanwhile, companies that once paid top dollar for original images now often turn to stock photo agencies to meet their photography needs for a small fraction of what it would cost to hire a pro.

Plus, with the readership of printed newspapers and magazines on the decline, there are fewer job opportunities for photojournalists (although digital news outlets saw a solid bump in online subscriptions after the 2016 election). According to the U.S. Bureau of Labor Statistics, there is an 8 percent projected decline in photography-related jobs through 2026, but there are still viable career opportunities for professional photographers in areas such as portrait, commercial, and event photography.

As you're choosing a photography specialty to pursue, make sure there's a demand for it where you plan to live or work. For example, if you live in a rural area, the demand for a commercial or real estate photographer may be limited, but there may be plenty of opportunity for portrait, wedding, and/or event photographers, assuming the region doesn't have too much competition from fellow photographers.

Despite what seems to be an uphill battle trying to find success as a professional photographer, especially with the competition you'll face from other photographers and the shrinking demand for many photography specialties, a lot comes down to being able to develop your own niche, identifying a market in your geographic area, and creating a unique photography style that your potential customers and clients will be willing to pay for and perceive to have a premium value. Being able to market yourself successfully (in the real world and online) to your target audience has also become a must-have skill that you'll need to develop.

# Photographer Specialty Areas

The field of photography is probably more diverse than you think. For photographers with a defined interest and talent, and who use a bit of creativity, there are many viable specialties worth exploring. Some of the more popular specialties are described in this chapter, but by tapping your imagination and doing some research to determine demand in your geographic area, you're likely to discover other viable opportunities.

For example, there are people who earn an excellent part- or full-time salary working as a pet photographer, while others have chosen a niche focusing on drone photography catering to the real estate market. Instead of traditional event or wedding photography, you might focus on shooting bar mitzvahs; school plays or concerts; local school-related sporting events; or events held by local dance, karate, or acting schools.

Let's look at some of the more popular photography specialties that have traditionally allowed professional photographers to earn a respectable income.

## *Fine Art Photography*

Fine art photography is for the creative individual who enjoys taking pictures for their aesthetic value—landscapes, nature, wildlife, nudes, or portraits. These high-quality images are often categorized as works of art that are sometimes displayed and sold in galleries, with prints reproduced in limited editions for collectors, dealers, and curators. Many fine art photos also appear in books for the general public.

Collectors also have a special interest in fine art photography books because they are usually limited editions with a short print run and no reprints. Fine art images are sometimes printed on note cards, calendars, and posters (all potential revenue generators), although some collectors would consider those to be "inferior" products.

Fine art photography is truly in the eye of the beholder—or camera. Some people think anything that is worthy of framing and hanging on a wall should be classified as fine art. But many artists would cringe at that interpretation. The question of whether photography is art has been disputed for decades, and it really comes down to:

1.  Its visual appeal
2.  The photographer's perception

3. The public's opinion
4. The presentation of the images

**stat fact**

The most expensive photograph ever sold was made by German visual artist Andreas Gursky in 1999. In 2011, his print of *Rhein II* was auctioned by Christie's of New York for $4.3 million.

In today's modern world, a successful fine art photographer must build a demand for their work and attract a loyal customer base. In addition to having an abundance of creative talent as a fine art photographer, strong marketing and branding skills are essential. You'll also need to develop long-term relationships with galleries, auction houses, and other places that will showcase and potentially sell your work. Having a well-designed and professional looking online presence that appeals to the target audience for your work is also essential.

Discover places to showcase your work at local and regional art fairs and events, as well as in galleries, restaurants, contemporary art museums, and other venues that are willing to display the work of up-and-coming fine art photographers. Based on where you live, this will require some research and creativity on your part.

## Photojournalism

Photojournalism is the ability to tell a story through images of a particular subject, at a specific location, or of an occasion. The photographer shoots the scenario happening around them, without interfering in any way—in other words, no staged or formal shots. A photojournalist might be called on to shoot a crime scene, a newsworthy event, or images that'll go along with an article being published in a newspaper, magazine, or on a website, for example.

A photojournalist needs to hustle and be extremely observant. It's essential to be in the right location, at the right moment, and be able to capture what's happening in the most attention-getting and visually descriptive way possible. Photojournalism is not just about taking the best picture. It's about successfully being able to tell visually compelling stories in shooting situations where you have zero control over your subject(s), location, timing, or lighting. There are no do-overs and no way to direct your subjects. Being in the right place at the right time and capturing important moments is what photojournalism is all about.

Editorial photojournalism is used to present news material and events, which means photographers are constantly on the move and need to make instantaneous decisions. This can sometimes be a risky business if the photographer finds themselves in the middle of a police standoff, a natural disaster, or in the heart of a war zone, for example. This type of work can also be heart-wrenching, especially when photographing scenes immediately following a tragedy, and your job is to impartially capture the impact of a disaster and its victims.

The candid style of the photojournalist is also becoming very popular in commercial photography and is now used regularly at events, such as weddings, birthday parties, bar mitzvahs, corporate functions, charity events, or other social functions.

Photojournalists need to develop the ability and good judgment to objectively present an impartial, unbiased, and accurate narrative. In other words, the photojournalist must tell the truth as it unfolds. If they attempt to manipulate the scene in any way—even something as simple as moving two people closer together—then the truth has been altered.

## *Wedding and Special Event Photography*

Wedding and special event photography is for the individual who enjoys working with people and who wants to help them celebrate one of the most memorable days of their lives. Most of the work is done on location, although some photographers have studios for bridal portraits and engagement photos.

This may be surprising to some, but wedding photography is one of the trickiest areas of photography. Children's portrait photographer Alexi Killmer explains that the first wedding she photographed was one of the most challenging moments of her professional career. "This is when I learned that weddings are not for me. Having a second shooter is always good to have," she said.

Because so much might be happening during a wedding (or event), at any given time, working with a second shooter allows the photographers to be in two places at once and capture all the important moments happening around them.

During a wedding, bar mitzvah, party, or any corporate event, the photographer has very limited time to take as many shots as possible. Some of these shots will be candid, but it's also the photographer's responsibility to capture posed shots of the bride and groom, as well as close family members, friends, and other attendees.

In wedding photographs, everyone needs to be smiling and look beautiful, and it's the photographer's job to ensure the right collection of images are taken that feature the appropriate people together. As all experienced photographers know, things never go as planned at weddings and events, so the photography must be able to adapt. Things get even trickier when it rains on the day of a planned outdoor wedding, the festivities are moved indoors, and the ambient lighting leaves a lot to be desired.

A good photographer will not only be able to artfully capture treasured moments, but will also help the wedding party relax and have fun during the ceremony and festivities. A grumpy photographer who is curt and short-tempered will not get many referrals, no matter how talented they are.

That's why people skills and patience are a must for wedding and event photographers. These skills will be put to the ultimate test when you need to deal with the occasional overly demanding bride or groom, emotional parents, and/or drunk relatives who refuse to take direction when you're trying to take posed portraits. After all, one person in a group photo who is looking in the wrong direction, or who refuses to smile, will ruin an entire image.

Wedding photographers typically follow a pre-created shot list, which includes a selection of carefully scripted poses for ring exchanges, cake cutting, and bouquet tossing, for example. These formal, staged memories are very much a part of the wedding album package. However, a new genre of wedding photography has emerged: wedding photojournalism. This is an approach to shooting the big day emphasizing a candid documentary style of photography.

To help set the standards and advance the field, the Wedding Photojournalist Association (www.wpja.com) has stepped up to provide resources for "professional photographers skilled in the documentation of weddings and events in a candid, unobtrusive style." The group dates the style to the mid-20th century, when working photojournalists set the tone shooting high-profile brides, such as Grace Kelly and Marilyn Monroe.

The traditional, formal style will always be a mainstay for weddings, but that should not be the only style used. A wedding photographer should have a unique, defined style that differentiates their work from their competition. Today's couples are not going to be influenced by someone's superior lighting and posing capabilities—they want originality and images that are "Instagram-worthy."

**aha!**

Incorporate an artistic blend converting some full-color wedding images into black and white, then digitally hand color certain areas, like the flowers. Try different lenses, lens filters, and image editing techniques to achieve unusual, attention-grabbing, and visually pleasing results. Be creative!

The more skilled you become working with powerful photo editing and image enhancement software, such as Photoshop, the more flexibility you'll have when it comes to transforming your images into visually stunning, original, and attention-grabbing photos that your clients will cherish, truly appreciate, and share.

And that's how today's wedding photographers are distinguishing themselves in a growing field. Ray Strawbridge thinks some of the most successful photographers are those who do weddings and portraits. "As much as I hate to think of photography as a commodity, you have to find a service that people need or strongly desire," he states. "Regardless of what the economy is like—how much gas costs or who is unemployed—if there is a wedding, someone is going to be hired and paid to take pictures."

Strawbridge also feels this is one of the easiest niches to get started in, although the work itself can be challenging, grueling, and stressful. A photographer could start by shooting weddings on weekends and later add bridal portraits to the business. A natural offspring would be to offer other types of portraiture, such as children, pets, and families.

## Portraiture

Portraiture is the art of recording people (and sometimes pets or objects) at their best, be it through a painting, sculpture, or photography. Portrait photography has become a wide-ranging commercialized area because so many people enjoy having portraits made

### ► A Special Kind of Photographer

Children's photography is one of the fastest-growing segments in portraiture, and there are many ways to narrow this field down to a finely tuned niche. Karen Dórame discovered this by accident. She cofounded Special Kids Photography of America (SKPA), a nonprofit organization that trains photographers to work with children who have special needs and disabilities. The organization was born out of Dórame's frustration of being unable to find a professional who was comfortable photographing her special needs child.

The organization has trained hundreds of photographers nationwide on how to work effectively with special needs children. These trained photographers can then use the SKPA accreditation and logo when advertising and marketing their photography business. For more information about this organization, visit: www.specialkidsphotography.com.

Even if you are not planning to work with special needs children in your niche, this type of training can still be invaluable. An example would be photographing a family reunion or wedding with a special needs child, in attendance, and being able to make everyone feel comfortable while taking some great shots.

to commemorate special events like births, milestone birthdays, family reunions, weddings, anniversaries, and graduations.

When it comes to taking professional-quality portraits, not only do you need the right camera equipment, but you'll need to maintain full control over lighting and the entire setting. At the same time, you'll need to direct your subject(s), show them how to pose, provoke the appropriate facial expression, and most important, make them feel at ease in front of the camera. Your communication and interpersonal skills are as important as your photography skills.

Today's portrait photographers are no longer happy simply portraying someone's likeness in the traditional, posed style. They want to capture their subjects' personalities and stamp something of their essence onto the photograph. This is why a lot of portrait photographers go outside the studio and take photographs in natural settings, such as outdoors or in the home or business of the individual. You should have a working knowledge of photo-friendly outdoor spaces that are not only visually appealing, but also open to the public (or that you have permission to use as a backdrop). If you do location shoots, you should also be ready to travel with your "portable studio" that includes scenic backdrops and lighting equipment.

One professional photographer who knows how to work on location is Michael Weschler. Having produced a lot of celebrity portraits, he enjoys combining his talent for shooting interiors with big personalities. "Clearly, these are not real moments, but I want to give viewers the feeling that these are real people in real settings," he explained. For example, if someone is in their living room, Weschler is not going to have them wear an evening gown. Instead, you may see them playing with their dog, sitting at the piano, or just walking in from making an espresso in the kitchen.

**aha!**

Most portrait photographers agree that you need a good, sturdy tripod to keep the camera stable and a cable release (or wireless/remote release system) that will allow you to click the shutter without touching the camera. Just as important is having a nice selection of backgrounds on hand as well as a proper lighting/flash setup.

Next, as a portrait photographer, you'll need to develop specialized skills when it comes to editing and enhancing your images. In addition to the gold standard Adobe Photoshop, there are software applications, such as PortraitPro (www.portraitprofessional.com), that give you access to incredibly powerful portrait editing tools that are easy to use and designed to reduce and streamline your image editing responsibilities while consistently achieving highly professional results.

"I think there is a difference between creating a moment vs. contriving it and having it feel artificial. It's important to be as realistic as possible," he adds.

Photographers in the portraiture business need to learn what types of pictures sell best, based on who their clients are. For example, the picture of a frilly dressed 3-year-old looking demurely down at her posies may be great for a calendar or poster, but her parents will most likely buy the close-up shot of her smiling, cherubic face.

Learning the art of posing your subjects for portraits is an important skill to master. There are plenty of how-to photography books and entire photography classes dedicated to the art of posing and lighting subjects for portraits. This also takes a lot of practice and the ability for the photographer to communicate calmly and clearly with their subjects. The best-looking poses for a portrait are often uncomfortable and unnatural for the subject, which is why the photographer needs to offer clear direction and constant assurances.

In addition to arranging subjects to their best advantage, a portrait photographer also has to charm them into feeling their best. The subject's facial expression and body language will dramatically impact the appearance of a portrait. The more relaxed and comfortable the subject(s) feel, the better the end results will be. This means a portrait photographer needs to be a "people person," while simultaneously working with their camera gear, setting, and lighting in order to orchestrate the perfect shots.

## Pet Photography

People's passion for pets has led to increased opportunities for photographers. Pet photography has taken a prominent place in the pet service industry, and pet owners are often willing to spend more for a pet portrait than they are for a portrait of their children.

According to the American Pet Products Association (APPA), Americans spent more than $72.13 billion on their pets in 2018 alone. This included services such as dog walking, obedience training, grooming, and pet photography. Depending on location and clientele, typical sitting fees for pets range from $50 to $200, with photo packages priced $200 to $1,000.

In addition to selling customers traditional prints of their pets, selling products featuring pet photos are also popular and potentially profitable. Consider selling your pet portraits on clothing, coffee mugs, smartphone/tablet covers, and greeting cards. You can also offer enlarged canvas or metal prints at premium prices.

If you live in a rural area, your work as a pet photographer can go beyond just shooting cats and dogs. You can opt to specialize in livestock and farm animals (like horses). One way to promote your pet photography business is to team up with local groomers, trainers, dog walkers, pet sitters, and veterinarians. You can also donate your time to provide pet photography to animal shelters in exchange for promotional mentions.

Yet another option for attracting attention to your work is to participate in photography competitions hosted at state fairs and/or 4-H shows, for example. Winning these competitions not only boosts your credibility, but it also allows you to reach potential new customers and clients and in some cases, sell copies of your work to attendees. You can also maximize your expertise with the fair and show-animal demographic by partnering with county and state fairs to serve as the official photographer for the winner's circle at animal and livestock shows. Most fairs offer professional photographs for participants to order, and many of those photos are featured in fair-related publications, which reach a wide audience of ranchers, farmers, 4-H families, and show animal enthusiasts.

Some pet photographers set up a fixed location studio. Those who tend to be more successful, however, have a mobile studio and travel to their client's location or schedule "pet photography days" at local grooming facilities or dog parks. Of course, you need to be comfortable working with animals and be able to help pets relax in front of the camera.

Before delving into a pet photography business, consider taking some basic dog training and animal behavior classes so you learn how to safely work with animals. Learn to identify when an animal is scared, which could cause them to attack (if they get frightened by a camera's flash or the click of the shutter, for example).

## Special Occasion (Noncorporate) Event Photography

Event photography is pretty much self-descriptive. You are capturing events as they unfold, at family events, proms, political or sporting events, pet shows, school events, or business functions—basically wherever the action is. However, event photography is also a very broad term, and you should narrow your specialty to include no more than two or three types of events that you specialize in. The more specialized your niche is, the better.

Although you will see and hear the terms "photojournalistic" and "documentary" used interchangeably in event photography, the two styles are quite different. The most prevalent style is documentary, which is a presentation of the facts that includes portraits, classic formals, and still life shots, along with candid moments. A photojournalistic style is the telling of a story through pictures, with no interference from or staged shots by the photographer.

Photographing an event can be a challenge. It's not always practical to use a flash, but shooting in natural or ambient light can sometimes be tricky. Using a flash can be distracting or even prohibited at some events.

You're also going to be moving around a lot, so travel lightly with only the essentials in your case (don't forget backup batteries and memory cards). Wear dark clothing so that you can blend into the background and remain as inconspicuous as possible. Get as much information as you possibly can before attending the event to help you anticipate where you need to be and when.

Based on the type(s) of event photography you specialize in, having the right selection of camera(s), lenses, lighting equipment, and related gear is essential. You should also create your own customized shot list prior to each event so you have a plan for what types of shots you'll need to take based on requests or the needs of your clients. At the very least, think about your shooting goals in advance and plan accordingly.

## Additional Niche Photography Fields

The following is information about additional photography specialties that you might choose to pursue. This is by no means a comprehensive list. It's just a sampling of the types of photography-related opportunities you might become interested in. Each requires a unique skill set as well as the right collection of photography equipment and related gear.

Some of these opportunities or career paths require training, or even some type of accreditation or formal education as well as proven experience. After all, no advertising agency is going to hire you if you don't already have an extensive portfolio of work showcasing your talents as a commercial photographer, for example. Check out these great niches:

▶ *Advertising and commercial photography.* Freelance photographers are typically employed by an agency or company to take pictures for ads, catalogs, brochures, product packaging, newsletters, websites, social media feeds, etc.

▶ *Aerial photography.* Images taken from the air (such as a drone, helicopter, plane, hot air balloon, or specially rigged kite) are used for military purposes, commercial advertising, land use planning, environmental studies, and real estate marketing, for example. Drone photography has become a niche photography opportunity that when done well, can lead to nice profits. Of course, you'll need to invest in a drone with a good camera mounted to it, then perfect your drone-piloting skills.

▶ *Architectural and industrial photography.* This specialty is ideal for the individual who appreciates structural design. Photographers must be skilled in taking both interior and exterior shots. This is considered a separate specialty than real estate photography.

▶ *Catalog and website photography.* This involves shooting specific product images, sometimes with special equipment and techniques. There are different styles of product photography. Your client might want a product showcased in a handful of close-up images to depict extreme detail, while using a simple, solid color background and perfect lighting (with no shadows). These shots are typically created in a studio setting, using a lightbox, for example. There's also an ongoing demand for lifestyle product photography, which showcases products being used in the real world.

▶ *Fashion photography.* This specialty is a cross between commercial and portrait photography. Fashion photographs are used for magazines, ads, catalogs, and websites, and are displayed in retail stores, for example. For this type of work, the subject is typically the clothing, makeup, or accessories, as opposed to the attractive model.

▶ *Food photography.* Images made for restaurants, supermarkets, and food companies are used for promotion in posters, ads, circulars, magazines, websites, and menus, for example. Shooting food images for cookbooks is also part of this niche.

▶ *Forensic and evidence photography.* Photograph crime scenes and autopsies for scientists and law enforcement agencies.

▶ *Nature and wildlife photography.* This niche is perfect for someone who enjoys the outdoors as well as photographing wild animals, landscapes, and wildlife.

▶ *Photographic analysis.* This field requires studying and analyzing images to determine if they have been altered or tampered with.

▶ *Portfolio photography.* Artists, corporations, singers, models, and actors need photographs of their work or themselves for presentations. Every actor, for example, needs professional headshots that showcase their looks and personality in a specific way that'll appeal to casting directors.

▶ *Public relations photography.* Photographers are hired to promote businesses or individuals by taking pictures at documented and prearranged events, such as trade shows or press conferences. You may also be hired to take product shots or portraits of company executives.

▶ *Real estate photography.* Most of these pictures are used by high-end Realtors and real estate agents for showcasing and selling residential and commercial real estate properties. Images might ultimately be printed in ads or used online. In addition to traditional real estate photography, there's a growing demand for showcasing properties using 360-degree images (for use on websites) as well as drone photography (which also falls under the niche of aerial photography mentioned earlier).

▶ *School photography.* This type of photography covers class portraits, sports team photographs, teacher portraits, graduations, etc. Most schools hire a company that handles all of its photography needs, so you'll need to market yourself to school system officials and be able to pass a background check, since you'll be working directly with kids and teens.

▶ *Scientific and technical photography.* Photographers need to understand and illustrate the subject they are photographing. The pictures can be used for research, presentations, education, and other purposes. Photographers are usually in-house and rarely freelance.

▶ *Sports photography.* A subset of event photography, this niche comes with the best seats in the house. With this adventure comes the danger of being squashed by a linebacker while capturing the perfect catch on film. The more you know about the sport you're shooting, the better, because you'll be able to anticipate when the perfect photo opportunities are about to happen. As a sports photographer, being at the right place at the right moment and ready to shoot with the most appropriate type of lens is a skill you'll need to master.

▶ *Travel photography.* This is great for individuals who enjoy being on the road, but beware this niche is very competitive. Again, you'll need to capture a wide range of indoor and outdoor locations, often in less-than-ideal shooting situations, but make the locales look amazing.

▶ *Underwater photography.* Photographers should be excellent swimmers with scuba diving skills and special underwater camera equipment.

The various fields of photography often complement and segue into each other. Many photographers feel comfortable shooting in two or three specialties. If you look at the work of the photographers profiled within this book, most have more than one specialty area, but all have a comprehensive and professional-looking portfolio available online that nicely showcases their specialty work.

# Market Research

Once you have chosen your niche or specialty, you will need to do an in-depth examination of your market. This assessment is essential to your success because it will provide you with information that helps you identify and reach your targeted audience as well as solve or avoid potential marketing problems.

Decide on the geographic area you want to serve, then determine if there are enough potential customers or clients in that area who meet your customer profile and allow you to generate an ongoing and respectable income. For instance, you may want to carve a niche in sports photography, but your area does not support any pro teams or large colleges and universities. In that case, you have two choices: You can either change the targeted geographic area or your strategy and focus on youth leagues and local high school games while you gain some valuable experience. This also gives you an opportunity to build your portfolio and expand your network of contacts.

Conducting market research also gives you information about your competitors. You need to find out what they're doing and how it meets—or doesn't meet—the needs of the market. One of the most basic elements of effective marketing is differentiating yourself from the competition. One marketing consultant calls it "eliminating the competition," because if you set yourself apart by doing something no one else does, then you essentially have no competition.

**tip**

Michael Weschler believes it's important to keep a balance and have some diversity as a photographer. He explains, "There is a danger in saying, 'I'm only going to do this specific type of work,' because you may have a dry spell. It might help to have something else going on, too."

You also need to know what your competition charges for services similar to what you plan to offer, make sure there's not too much direct competition in the area, and avoid getting into a price war that will result in you earning less profit (or no profit) in order to offer competitive pricing. Whenever possible, you're better off offering premium-level services and charging premium rates that you can justify based on the quality of your work.

Before you can differentiate yourself, you need to understand who your competitors are and why your customers might patronize them. Offering something no one else is offering could give you an edge in the market (if there's a demand), but it could also mean that someone else has tried that and it didn't work. Don't make hasty decisions. Do your homework before finalizing your service offerings or specialty. Use the Photographer's Niche Worksheet (see Figure 2–1 on page 25) to help you define your target market.

## Photographer's Niche Worksheet

How well have you defined your target market? This worksheet can help you get organized and coordinate your efforts:

Identify three specialty areas you would like to target:

1. _____

_____

2. _____

_____

3. _____

_____

What skills do you have in those areas?

_____

_____

_____

Will you need additional training or education?

_____

_____

What additional equipment will you need?

_____

_____

Do you have an already established and impressive portfolio of work that nicely showcases your skills related to your chosen specialty? If not, how long will it take you to create a portfolio? _____

_____

_____

_____

FIGURE 2–1: **Photographer's Niche Worksheet**

# Photographer's Niche Worksheet

Identify your target clients and their average budget to hire a photographer:

_____

_____

What services do they need? _____

_____

_____

Who is your competition (and how much competition will you face)? _____

_____

_____

How will your services be different? _____

_____

_____

Is your geographical location favorable to your business? _____

_____

_____

Do you (or will you) have a website or online presence that will appeal to your target audience? _____

_____

_____

What specialized and cost-effective advertising, marketing, and promotions (in the real world and online) will you do that will allow you to promote your photography services to your target audience? Do you have the resources, knowledge, and budget to manage ongoing campaigns that will allow you to reach customers and clients interested in hiring you, based on your specialty? _____

_____

_____

FIGURE 2–1: **Photographer's Niche Worksheet,** continued

# Taking Stock or Working on Assignment

n the early-to-mid 1900s, stock photography images were basically leftovers from various commercial assignments, commonly referred to as "outtakes" or "seconds." Stock image libraries and agencies cataloged and published the images pretty much the same way any other product catalog did with their merchandise and sold them for purchase and republication in ads, books, annual reports, and the like.

As time passed, customers came to realize they could save considerable time and money by using stock images instead of hiring a photographer for a specific assignment. Stock agencies endeavored to meet the increasing demands by trying to foresee their customers' needs and communicating them to photographers. By the 1980s, stock photography had become a specialty in its own right, with many photographers enjoying the flexibility of shooting stock instead of working on assignment. The industry remained competitive and today, thanks to the proliferation of online consumerism and marketing, stock imagery is a multibillion-dollar business. As a stock photographer, you'll be paid based on residual income (royalties), or in some cases, rights to your images will be purchased outright.

**tip**

To discover what's involved in having your work represented, along with more than 200,000 other photographers, by Getty Images and its subsidiaries, visit: www.gettyimages.com/workwithus. To get started offering your images through a stock agency, consider first submitting your work to smaller agencies.

Many photographers try to do both stock and assignment photography, although they usually prefer one over the other. In recent years, the stock imagery business has become very competitive, and the prices companies are willing to pay for stock photography has decreased rather dramatically. Thus, unless you have a vast collection of images being offered by stock agencies, and your photos are selected often for use by their clients, this will more realistically be a way to supplement your income as opposed to generate a full-time (or even a respectable part-time) income.

One of the most successful stock photo agencies is called Getty Images (www.gettyimages.com). It's among the world's leading creators and distributors of award-winning still imagery, video, music, and multimedia products as well as other forms of premium digital content, available through its trusted house of brands including iStock (www.istockphoto.com).

Using advanced search and image recognition technology, Getty Images serves more than 1.5 million business customers in over 100 countries. Images acquired from Getty Images help their customers produce work that appears every day in the world's most influential newspapers, magazines, advertising campaigns, films, television programs, books, and online media.

For each license for an image a customer purchases, photographers earn a royalty, which is a percentage of the price paid by the customer. Earnings vary, but according to Getty Images, "The more content you have in your portfolio that customers need, the more opportunities you'll have to gain earnings."

The opportunity to sell stock images is as vast as the locations where you will find those images used. They are often featured within all forms of advertising, as well as within brochures, billboards, presentations, books, magazines, product packaging, blogs, and websites. Stock images are routinely used by many commercial and nonprofit entities, such as architectural and design firms; advertising agencies; book, newspaper, magazine, website, and blog publishers; corporations in all industries; educational institutions; and website designers and graphic artists.

# How Stock Work Is Managed and Monetized

During the 1980s, photographers controlled all rights (copyrights) for their images. Then in the new millennium, royalty-free images with unlimited usage rights were introduced through large stock agencies. In today's market, stock photographers are faced with the struggle of accepting a flat, royalty-free fee, or sometimes retaining royalty control rights over their images.

Unfortunately, the battle is weighing heavily on the royalty-free side, which often means less revenue for the photographer. This newer model is replacing the rights-controlled version by offering a huge selection of images to buyers at significantly reduced prices.

It helps to understand the difference between royalty-free and rights-managed stock. Royalty-free does not actually mean "free," but it gives buyers permission to use the image multiple times in any number of ways, for as long as they want—for a one-time fee. There's usually a limit on how many times the image can be reproduced by a client.

The biggest downside for stock photography users is that they do not own the royalty-free image. Anyone—including competitors—can potentially use the same image, for the same fee, at the same time, and for the same purposes.

Images that are licensed, or "rights-managed," charge a fee each time an image is used. The buyer can have exclusive use for a limited time, allowing the photographer or agency to sell the image again when the embargo period is up. Fees are negotiable and are based on factors such as exclusivity, distribution (readership), how long it will be used, and where it will be used (region or country).

Although some photographers receive assignments for stock photos, it's more common for a photographer to take the images on their own and submit them later for possible presentation and representation by a stock photo agency. Working with a stock agency can be a lot of work. For it to be a financially lucrative opportunity, you'll need to provide hundreds of pictures, only a few of which customers of the stock agencies may want to license. As the photographer, you're also hidden behind a veil of anonymity: the "agency." As a result, the buyers don't know who you are, and you rarely get photo credit for your work.

Due to many stock agencies now offering millions of images online, prices for their customers to license or purchase images has dropped significantly in recent years, so if you're planning to make selling stock photography a cornerstone of your photography career, keep in mind this aspect of the business is no longer as lucrative as it once was. Instead, you might consider offering stock images through an agency or service as just one part of your overall photography business.

## How Profitable Is Stock Photography?

The profitability margin for stock photography varies widely. Images can sell for as little as $1 or as much as $2,500, depending on the client and how the image will be used. A photographer can send in 100 images and hope the stock agency will choose at least a dozen or more, assuming they meet the agency's technical, resolution, and file-size requirements. Depending on the contractual arrangements, the photographer can be paid per image or per usage.

## ▶ What Is Metadata?

Metadata is text-based information that gets linked with a digital image that becomes searchable. Your digital camera automatically records the date and time a photo was taken, as well as details about the camera settings used. Some digital cameras also capture the exact location (GPS coordinates) where images are shot.

In addition, with photo editing software and/or certain online services used for showcasing photos online, photographers can add additional metadata to an image, including a copyright message, title, caption, and a listing of keywords that describe the image and its contents.

Anytime someone uses an online search tool to find images, they're more likely to see your images in their search results if the title, caption, and keywords you use accurately and comprehensively describe your photos.

Adding metadata, including a title, caption, and keywords, to each of your images can be a time-consuming task, but if you're relying on people being able to find your images online, this is necessary and important.

Although the initial payout from some stock photo agencies average less than $1 per image, many photographers find this opportunity to be an attractive one because they can make money on photos they've already shot, without doing any marketing or selling themselves. A large portfolio with quality photographs of popular subject matters, combined with relevant titles, descriptions, keywords, and appropriate metadata, will greatly increase your chances of success. Stock photo agencies regularly publish guidelines that describe the types of images their clients are seeking. It's a good idea to study this information prior to submitting your work to stock photo agencies for evaluation.

Photos that are going to have a significantly larger audience need to have a higher level of exclusivity than what many stock photo agencies offer. For example, if a client wants a picture of a child at a birthday party for a PowerPoint presentation, they are not going to care who else uses it. However, if the client wants the picture exclusively for a national print ad campaign, for use on its website, or within a printed brochure, for example, those customers are willing to pay more, which means as the photographer, you'll earn more.

It's important to understand that commercial stock photographers are not phasing out; they are simply reconstructing and streamlining their specialty areas. The quality stock agencies that supply images for business-related clients (where the real money is) are specific and selective about the photographers and material they want to represent and offer to their clients.

## Working on Assignment

Assignment photography is when a photographer is commissioned to do a specific project by a client—advertising, weddings, portraiture, or any other event. This continues to be the most predominant and favored way of doing business today.

Unlike stock photography, which is shot in anticipation of being sold, work does not commence on the assignment until a contract has been negotiated and the photographer is in receipt of the advance fee. In addition to fees, the photographer working on assignment can sometimes also expect to be reimbursed for specific types of expenses.

Under terms of the contract, specifications, fees, and deadlines are worked out in advance. Every contract should include:

▶ An overall description of the project
▶ The start date for the project
▶ The deadline for completion

## ▶ Tips for Stock Photographers

As a photographer, it's important to find a niche in which to specialize. You want to become well known for that imagery and have a vast collection of work to showcase within your portfolio. You also want to avoid shooting subjects that are too generic or saturated in the market. Here are some other tips that may be useful:

▶ Use photo editing and image enhancement software, like Photoshop, to breathe new life into old images. This saves time and is less costly than reshooting. However, pay attention to a stock agency's strict guidelines about the types of enhancements that can be made to images before submitting them.

▶ When possible, work with an agency that allows you to interact with the client. Often when this happens and a buyer is looking for a specific picture, the project turns into an assignment. Large stock photo agencies typically don't allow this direct interaction, however.

▶ Work with an agency that does not require you to sign over exclusivity, giving them sole rights to an image. Avoid work-for-hire arrangements.

▶ Stock images need to be carefully organized. It's essential that each digital file has the specific types of metadata required by the stock agency (see "What Is Metadata?" on page 30). You'll also be required to provide detailed descriptions and keywords for the images you submit.

▶ A description of the images required by the client and what forms those images will take

▶ How many images will be delivered and in what format

▶ How, when, and where the images will be used

▶ Which party will retain copyright ownership of the image(s)

▶ What editing work/image enhancement will be included

▶ What expenses will be reimbursed to the photographer

▶ All fees to be paid to the photographer and when payment is due

Licensing terms for the images also need to be reviewed and negotiated. Most photographers prefer to sell limited rights, maintaining some control and ownership of the images. Of course, the more exclusive the rights, the higher the fee.

If a client buys all rights or a project is done on a work-for-hire basis, the client will own and be able to use the images in any conceivable way, preventing competitors from having the same or similar images. Both prohibit the photographer from using those images again.

An alternative to granting exclusivity to the client is to offer limited rights, ensuring the image will not be made available for use in certain markets without the client's consent. This approach still allows the photographer to resell the image in a noncompetitive market, either immediately or at some point in the future.

# The Digital Revolution

Film cameras were first introduced in the late 1880s, and they enjoyed over 100 years as being the primary way professional photographers took pictures. In the early 2000s, professional-level digital SLR cameras almost entirely replaced film cameras. While Kodak, for example, once dominated the film and film camera industries and was a brand that was synonymous with photography itself, the company never fully adapted to the digital photography age. Like Polaroid, Kodak has been replaced by companies like Nikon, Canon, Leica, Fujifilm, Panasonic, Olympus, Hasselblad, and Sony, which are pioneers leading the field.

Following in the footsteps of digital SLR cameras, the next big technological era of photography began with the introduction of full-frame, mirrorless digital cameras. These offer an even higher resolution than digital SLR cameras (with resolutions upwards of 50MP) and are quickly becoming the go-to cameras used by the pros. Some photographers still shoot with film but primarily for fine art projects.

As you should already know if you're planning to pursue photography as a career, MP stands for megapixels. One megapixel is equivalent to one million pixels, or individual colored dots that comprise an image. As a professional photographer, you typically want to shoot in the highest resolution possible. The higher the resolution of an image, the more fine-detail you'll see and the greater flexibility you'll have when editing. When you see a camera offering 50MP resolution, this means that each image can be comprised of up to 50 million pixels. If you'll be purchasing new camera equipment for your business, select a camera with the highest resolution you can afford.

Digital photography has transformed the traditional darkroom into a computer lab. But just because you're not working in a darkroom setting, this doesn't make processing digital images easier. In fact, the opposite is often true.

There are still just as many decisions to make when it comes to digitally editing and enhancing images shot with a digital camera. While most of your image management and editing may be done on a computer, the technology is now available to do professional-level editing on a tablet as well.

In mid to late 2019, for example, Adobe will release full-function versions of Photoshop, Lightroom, and other image editing and enhancement applications for the latest Apple iPad (and iPad Pro) models. These will offer a vastly more powerful tool set than Adobe's previous, scaled-down versions of its photography-related mobile applications.

In addition, some of the latest digital cameras have image enhancement tools built into the camera and allow for the easy (and fully automated) wireless transfer of images from the digital camera's memory card to a computer or cloud-based file storage service.

The camera, computer, and specialized photo editing and image enhancement software, along with software for organizing and managing digital image libraries, are everyday tools now used by pro photographers. Learning to use specialized photo editing and digital image enhancement applications is a skill set unto itself and a must for today's professional photographer.

## ▶ How Digital Cameras Differ

A *Digital SLR* (or *DSLR*) camera is a digital, single-reflex camera that uses interchangeable lenses. Within the camera body is a mirror used to reflect the light coming in from the lens so the light can be seen via an optical viewfinder.

Each time the camera's shutter button gets pressed and a digital photo is taken, the mirror flips out of the way, while at the same time, the shutter opens and allows the light that's coming through the lens to reach the camera's image sensor, which is used to create the digital image. A DSLR camera does not use film. The digital images are stored within a replaceable and reusable memory card that gets inserted into the camera.

A point-and-shoot digital camera typically lacks an optical viewfinder and does not use interchangeable lenses. These cameras tend to be used by amateurs as opposed to professional photographers.

A full-frame, mirrorless digital camera uses newer, cutting-edge technology and typically offers higher resolution shooting capabilities than even the highest-level DSLR cameras. This type of camera also typically uses interchangeable lenses but is mirrorless. The digital sensor within this type of camera replicates the format of 35mm film.

Released in March 2019, the Leica Q2 camera, retailing at around $4,995 (www.leicacamerausa. com), offers cutting-edge, full-frame, mirrorless technology and features shooting functionality and features sought after by pros. This camera has a noninterchangeable, fixed Summilux 28mm f/1.7 ASPH lens and a 47.3MP full-frame sensor. By the end of 2019, it's predicted that full-frame, mirrorless cameras from companies like Nikon and Canon will offer up to 70MP resolution (possibly higher).

Thus far, Nikon, Canon, Hasselblad, and Leica have been pioneers in the full-frame, mirrorless camera technology, which were introduced to the market in 2009 but didn't become commonly used by prosumer and professional photographers until around 2018.

As you make the decision to become a professional photographer, you might have a pro-level digital SLR camera with some high-end lenses at your disposal. These will likely continue to serve you well for the next several years. However, with improvements being made to full-frame, mirrorless digital cameras, and prices for this equipment slowly dropping, plan on upgrading your camera, lenses, and related gear within the next three to five years, at the latest.

If you're deciding to make the career move into professional photography and have not purchased your primary camera, consider investing in a full-frame, mirrorless digital camera, as opposed to one of the higher-end, pro-level digital SLR cameras. As you read earlier, this will soon be what the majority of professional photographers use, so it makes the most sense.

Choosing which pro-level digital camera equipment to shoot with is a matter of personal taste and budget, but once you settle on a camera brand, such as Nikon or Canon, you'll likely want to stick with that brand for many years to come since lenses between brands are not easily interchangeable. Nikon lenses work with Nikon cameras, and Canon lenses work with Canon cameras. Adapters are available, but there are significant drawbacks to using them.

Over time, you'll likely invest upwards of $5,000 to $10,000 (or more) on lenses for your digital camera(s). You'll want to use those lenses for many years to come, so it becomes more cost effective to occasionally upgrade just your camera body to a more technologically advanced model but keep using your existing lenses.

Keep in mind that lenses for full-frame, mirrorless digital cameras are different from those designed for digital SLR cameras. It makes sense to invest in equipment that is cutting edge now, but that will soon be commonplace, as opposed to investing in digital SLR camera(s) and lenses, which you know in the not-too-distant future will become outdated.

That being said, there are amazing deals to be found on used and refurbished, pro-level digital SLR cameras and equipment. The prices for this technology will continue to fall as it's replaced with full-frame, mirrorless digital camera technology. Thus, you need to think about the best way to invest your money in camera(s), lenses, and related equipment as you launch your professional photography business.

## stat fact

Because powerful digital cameras are now being built into smartphones and tablets, point-and-shoot and digital SLR camera sales among consumers have dropped 84 percent since 2010, according to The Statista (www.statista.com/chart/5782/digital-camera-shipments).

Meanwhile, in January 2019, Canon predicted a 50-percent plunge in digital camera sales over the next two years. As of early 2019, the global marker for interchangeable lens digital cameras was roughly 10 million units per year. Canon predicted that with the expansion of its prosumer and professional-level full-frame, mirrorless digital camera lineup, as well as the continued availability of digital SLR cameras targeted to the prosumer and professional-level audience, the demand for these cameras will be at least 5 to 6 million units per year moving forward.

One problem professional photographers face is that the demand for high-end digital cameras is dropping steadily, as consumer-oriented digital cameras (including those built into smartphones and tablets) have become more powerful and much less expensive. As a result, companies like Nikon and Canon are selling far fewer pro-level cameras than ever, which means prices are not falling as quickly as other technology-oriented products that have a growing (not shrinking) demand.

## Plan Your Camera Equipment Budget Intelligently

As a professional photographer, is it essential that you have a relatively cutting-edge digital camera (with compatible lenses and gear) as your primary shooting camera. In addition, you'll need to invest in a high-end desktop or laptop computer (or both, depending on your work habits). The computer will need a powerful graphics card, high-resolution (4K or higher) monitor, plenty of RAM memory, a fast processor, and a large hard drive.

Because digital camera resolutions continue to improve (some are now upwards of 50MP), this means that the file size of individual shots it also getting larger, especially if you shoot in the RAW file format. Your computer must be able to process, display, and manipulate these large digital image files without slowing down or crashing.

You'll also need to invest in a local backup storage option, such as a large, external hard drive that connects to your computer. Plus, there's an increasing need among photographers to also use a cloud-based file storage option to maintain a reliable backup and easily accessible archive of their entire digital image library. It's not uncommon for this library to exceed hundreds of thousands of separate high-resolution images over time. This same cloud-based service can be used as one option for sharing collections of high-resolution images with specific customers or clients.

Plan on upgrading your computer equipment every few years as technology improves, and know that your

**aha!**

There are many cloud-based services for backing up and storing digital image collections. Some, like iCloud, Microsoft OneDrive, and Google Photos, are targeted more to consumers. Others, which are discussed throughout this book, offer additional tools that are better suited to pro photographers.

Be sure to choose a cloud-based service that offers the collection of tools and security options you need, and understand there is almost always a monthly or annual subscription cost for using these services.

local and remote (cloud-based) file storage needs will increase, potentially exponentially, in the years to come. Plus, as the technological revolution continues, you'll likely want to go mobile, which will require you to have a high-end desktop computer when working from your home, office, or studio, as well as an equally powerful laptop computer (and/or tablet) when you need to work on location during or immediately after a shoot, for example.

Another technology-related purchase you'll want to consider is a high-end, wide-format (also referred to as large-format) digital photo printer so you can create prints and enlargements in-house, as needed, using top-quality photo paper and inks. While a standard photo printer can create prints up to 8.5 by 11 inches, a wide-format printer can create enlargements up to 24-, 36-, 44-, or 64-inches wide, depending on the printer make and model. You'll read more about choosing the right equipment in Chapter 8.

Use the Anticipated Technology Needs and Budget worksheet (see Figure 4–1 on page 41) to help you plan your technology-related budget when it comes to investing in or upgrading your camera and computer-related equipment.

## Consider All Your Supplementary Photography Equipment and Gear Needs

In addition to a primary shooting camera, it's always a good idea to have a backup, secondary camera on hand, especially during time-sensitive and important shoots where a reshoot or reschedule is not possible. Beyond your camera, depending on your chosen specialty and the requirements of your shoot, you'll likely need a wide range of other equipment and gear, which might include:

▶ Backdrops/backdrop stand
▶ Camera bag
▶ External storage device
▶ Extra camera batteries
▶ Extra memory cards
▶ Flash(es)
▶ Lens filters
▶ Lighting
▶ Multiple lenses
▶ Personal wifi hotspot. This allows you to create a wifi hotspot anywhere there's a cellular data connection, which can be used by many of the latest digital camera models to automatically upload images (as they're shot) to a cloud-based service. The Skyroam Solis ($149.99, www.skyroam.com/solis), for example, offers internet

## Anticipated Technology Needs and Budget

| Equipment | Description | Currently Own | Immediately Need | Future Investment | Cost |
|---|---|---|---|---|---|
| Primary Digital Camera | | __ Yes<br>__ No | __ Yes<br>__ No | __ Yes<br>__ No | $ |
| Secondary Digital Camera | | __ Yes<br>__ No | __ Yes<br>__ No | __ Yes<br>__ No | $ |
| Camera Lens #1 | | __ Yes<br>__ No | __ Yes<br>__ No | __ Yes<br>__ No | $ |
| Camera Lens #2 | | __ Yes<br>__ No | __ Yes<br>__ No | __ Yes<br>__ No | $ |
| Camera Lens #3 | | __ Yes<br>__ No | __ Yes<br>__ No | __ Yes<br>__ No | $ |
| Camera Lens #4 | | __ Yes<br>__ No | __ Yes<br>__ No | __ Yes<br>__ No | $ |
| Camera Lens #5 | | __ Yes<br>__ No | __ Yes<br>__ No | __ Yes<br>__ No | $ |
| Core Camera Gear (Flash, Tripod, etc.) | | __ Yes<br>__ No | __ Yes<br>__ No | __ Yes<br>__ No | $ |
| Desktop Computer | | __ Yes<br>__ No | __ Yes<br>__ No | __ Yes<br>__ No | $ |
| Laptop Computer | | __ Yes<br>__ No | __ Yes<br>__ No | __ Yes<br>__ No | $ |
| Tablet | | __ Yes<br>__ No | __ Yes<br>__ No | __ Yes<br>__ No | $ |
| High-Capacity External Hard Drive | | __ Yes<br>__ No | __ Yes<br>__ No | __ Yes<br>__ No | $ |
| High-Resolution (4K or Higher) Monitor | | __ Yes<br>__ No | __ Yes<br>__ No | __ Yes<br>__ No | $ |
| Wide Format Photo Printer | | __ Yes<br>__ No | __ Yes<br>__ No | __ Yes<br>__ No | $ |

FIGURE 4–1: **Anticipated Technology Needs and Budget**

## Anticipated Technology Needs and Budget

| Equipment | Description | Currently Own | Immediately Need | Future Investment | Cost |
|---|---|---|---|---|---|
| Photo Editing and Image Enhancement Software | | __ Yes<br>__ No | __ Yes<br>__ No | __ Yes<br>__ No | $ |
| Image Management Software or Other Specialty Software | | __ Yes<br>__ No | __ Yes<br>__ No | __ Yes<br>__ No | $ |
| Other | | | | | $ |
| Other | | | | | $ |
| Total Technology Budget | | | | | $ |

FIGURE 4–1: **Anticipated Technology Needs and Budget,** continued

connectivity for a flat daily or monthly fee. It works across the United States, as well as in hundreds of other countries with no international roaming charges.

► Props and set pieces

► Tripod or monopod

On the plus side, if you can't afford to buy all the needed equipment and gear outright, there are opportunities to rent. When choosing your equipment, think about how important portability is for you as a photographer. Will you be transporting everything from location to location or setting everything up and shooting at a fixed location, such as your studio?

When it comes to choosing lighting, backdrops, and set pieces, there are different options based on your portability and budgetary needs, so do your homework before making each purchase. As you'll discover, photography backgrounds come in a wide range of sizes and designs and are made from various materials (some of which are more rugged than others).

For example, paper backdrops are great for one-time use, but the wide paper rolls (up to 107 inches wide) are very difficult to travel with, unless you have a large vehicle. Cloth or vinyl backdrops can be folded or rolled, and are much more durable.

To discover all your photography backdrop, set, and prop options, check out these and other online businesses:

▶ Backdrop Express: www.backdropexpress.com

▶ Backdrop Outlet: www.backdropoutlet.com

▶ Denny Manufacturing: www.dennymfg.com

▶ NextDayFlyers: www.nextdayflyers.com/banner-printing/backdrops.php

▶ PhotoPie Backdrops: www.photopiebackdrops.com/Photography-Backdrops

## Embrace Technology

While it's true that most people are more tech-savvy than ever thanks to the growth of the smartphone and tablet market, that doesn't necessarily mean they are knowledgeable about how to use professional photography equipment. Becoming a professional photographer requires you to be tech-savvy. If you're not comfortable using technology, you're going to have a difficult time learning how to use your professional-level digital camera (which has its own operating system as well as its unique assortment of buttons, dials, menus, and commands based on the camera make and model).

Being able to figure out how to take professional-quality photos using your camera is just the first step. You then need to understand wireless technology enough so you can transfer images from your digital camera's memory card to your computer, mobile device, and/or a cloud-based service.

Your computer (or mobile device) will then be used to view, organize, edit, enhance, print, share, store, and archive your digital images. Thus, you'll need to download, install, and use the right collection of applications to handle your work flow needs and become proficient using those applications.

Since you'll definitely have to maintain an online presence as a pro photographer, you'll need to acquire the basic skills for creating and managing a website; creating and sharing online albums/galleries to showcase your images; and using social media to showcase your work and interact with current and potential customers/clients.

Depending on the photography specialties you pursue, you'll need to become a master at using lighting and flashes that are now often controlled wirelessly from your camera. It may also be necessary to learn how to operate a professional-level photo printer and/or pilot a drone that's equipped with a camera.

In fact, just about every facet or task associated with being a digital photographer requires working with technologies, understanding what those technologies are capable of, then using them to realize your artistic vision when it comes to taking, editing, enhancing, printing, and showcasing your work.

Along with using technology to handle photography-related tasks, you'll also need to rely on technology and specialized applications to handle your bookkeeping, invoicing, credit card payment processing, email, contact relationship management (CRM), appointment scheduling, and other common business-related tasks.

Beyond just working with your camera and computer locally, chances are you'll also need to develop an understanding of how to use at least one cloud-based service in a secure and productive way. These days, every computer and mobile device's operating system integrates with cloud-based services, and many of the specialty photography applications you'll be using rely on cloud services to back up, sync, archive, and share your digital images.

If you're not comfortable using technology in your everyday life, much less for professional purposes, before you consider pursuing a career as a professional photographer, take some classes and become proficient using digital cameras, computers, mobile devices, and the internet.

Technology may be intimidating, but if you learn at your own pace, it's not something you should be afraid of. In fact, you should learn to embrace technology and discover all the ways it can save you time, frustration, and money as you embark on your career as a professional photographer and begin your life as an entrepreneur.

# Focusing on the Right Path

Running your own photography business can be great fun, but it's about more than taking pictures and scouting locations for shoots. It also involves the nuts-and-bolts aspects of starting and running a legitimate business. One of the first steps involved in starting any new business is to develop a well-thought-out business plan. This can become your blueprint or roadmap for success. While a formal business plan is often used to help a startup recruit investors, as a small-business operator, you can create a business plan that simply allows you to outline and fine-tune your ideas. The process of composing a business plan and compiling the information to include within it forces you to think about all aspects of the business and will later help you stay focused.

You might think that the process of writing a formal business plan is a time-consuming and daunting task. However, it doesn't have to be, especially if you're not seeking investors or loans from a bank.

First, invest in some business plan creation software (or subscribe to an online-based business plan creation service), such as LivePlan (www.liveplan.com), Business Plan Pro (www.businessplanpro.com), or Growthink (https://strategicplantemplate.growthink.com). Any of these easy-to-use applications will walk you, step by step, through the business plan creation process. Or check out *Write Your Business Plan* (Entrepreneur Press, 2016) or *Start Your Own Business* (Entrepreneur Press, 2018).

Another option is to download a free business plan template from the SBA (www.sba.gov/business-guide/plan-your-business/write-your-business-plan) and use it to help gather your ideas, dreams, and goals and shape them into what will hopefully become the plan for a well-structured and eventually profitable business.

Writing a business plan forces you to sit down and consider a range of areas:

▶ Examining the financial aspects related to your business idea.
▶ Analyzing the potential risks.
▶ Formulating and fine-tune your goals and vision.
▶ Determining your strengths as a photographer and business professional.
▶ Pinpointing your weaknesses and what skills you still need to develop.
▶ Anticipating the challenges you'll face.
▶ Figuring out what types of assistance you'll need.
▶ Choosing your photography specialty.
▶ Analyzing your competition.
▶ Considering who your target audience (potential customers/clients) will be.
▶ Creating a step-by-step game plan for getting the business set up as a legal entity, then operational in a realistic time frame.
▶ Developing a marketing, advertising, and promotions strategy based on your goals, time constraints, and budget.

Working through the process of creating a business plan helps you ask some of the hard questions about how you are going to make your photography dreams a reality.

# Be a Fan of the Plan

If you're excited about your business, creating a business plan should be an exciting process, not a painful one. It will help you define and evaluate the overall feasibility of your concept, clarify your goals, and determine what you'll need for startup and long-term operations.

Once your business plan is created, it will serve as a detailed roadmap for the formation and operation of your company. You'll use it as a guide, referring to it regularly as you work through the startup process, then during your day-to-day business-related activities. And if you need to seek outside financing, either in the form of loans or investors, your business plan will be the tool that helps convince funding sources that you are worth every penny.

Putting together a business plan is not a linear process, although the final product may look that way. Take your time developing your plan. This is a very important first step in establishing what needs to become a strong foundation for your business.

## *Start with a Clear Mission Statement*

A mission statement is an important part of your business plan. In just a sentence or two, it needs to summarize your business and its objectives in a clear and concise way. As the business operator, you must develop a crystal-clear understanding of what the mission of your company will be. Your mission statement should answer these questions:

- ▶ What will you be doing and why?
- ▶ How and where will your business be conducted?
- ▶ Who will be your clientele?
- ▶ What will be unique about your business and its services?
- ▶ What will be your corporate philosophy, and why should people care?

Even if you have already started your photography business, it's not too late to write your mission statement. This helps everyone involved see the big picture and stay focused on the

**warning**

When you make a change to one part of your business plan, be sure you think through how that change will impact the rest of your operation. For example, if you start out working exclusively in a studio doing only portraitures but later decide to go out on location to shoot weddings and other events, you have to change your equipment needs, your scheduling plans, and your projected income as well as your marketing, advertising, and promotional plans.

After all, shooting weddings means you will be working on weekends, and you'll need to adopt different methods for finding and landing clients, compared to running a photo studio where people come to you for portraits.

true goals of the business. At a minimum, your mission statement should define who your primary customers are, identify the products and services you provide, and describe the geographical area(s) where you'll operate.

**aha!**

Your company's mission statement will be a big help when it comes to brainstorming an attention-getting advertising or marketing slogan that you can prominently place in a range of areas: your advertising and marketing materials, your website, your company's social media profiles, or your business cards and letterhead.

For example, your mission statement might state, "The mission of ABC Photography is to provide top-quality commercial photography, at a fair and reasonable price in the Raleigh/Durham area, while assuring that our clients will receive the highest level of attention, commitment, and professionalism."

Your mission statement should be short—usually just one sentence and certainly no more than two or three. Anything longer isn't a mission statement and may be too convoluted and hard to memorize. Your mission statement also doesn't have to be clever or catchy—just accurate. Don't make grandiose statements that you have no ability to achieve or create expectations that you can't or will not be able to live up to. The Mission Statement Worksheet will help you get a jump start on writing it (see Figure 5–1 on page 49).

Once you've articulated your message, communicate it as often as possible to employees, customers, suppliers, and potential investors and lenders.

## Time to Write the Plan

Once you've identified the products and services you want to offer and to whom and you have created a mission statement, you're ready to work on your business plan.

Though the specific content of your business plan will be as unique as the photography niche you choose, there is a basic format it should follow. The format ensures that you address all the issues you need to as well as provide lenders (and potential investors) with a comprehensive document that's organized in a familiar way.

Using text, as well as charts, tables, and perhaps a few photographs to demonstrate key points, the main parts of your business plan should include the components covered in Figure 5–2, Business Plan Elements, starting on page 50.

Nobody likes to admit their personal or professional shortcomings. However, your business plan should identify any weaknesses and, more important, describe how you plan to overcome them. For instance, if you're a great photographer but your photo editing and image enhancement skills are lacking, discuss how you're enrolled in an

## Mission Statement Worksheet

To develop an effective mission statement, answer these questions, then summarize your answers into a single sentence, using 200 words or less:

What type of photographic products and/or services do I plan to produce or offer? _____

_____

_____

In what geographical location will I operate my photography business? _____

_____

_____

Why does my company exist? Whom will it serve? What is our purpose? _____

_____

_____

_____

What are the strengths, weaknesses, opportunities, and threats? _____

_____

_____

Considering the above, along with my expertise and resources, what photography specialties should the business focus on? _____

_____

_____

What is important to me as a professional photographer? _____

_____

_____

_____

FIGURE 5–1: **Mission Statement Worksheet**

# Business Plan Elements

## Cover Sheet

The title at the top of the page should identify the document as a Confidential Business Plan. Further down the page, add your business name, address, phone number, email address, and website. Then list yourself as the owner or proprietor.

## Table of Contents

Start building your business plan by compiling a detailed table of contents as an outline. It will help you to think about the nuts and bolts in planning your business by serving as a guide during the process. Expand the table of contents by adding subsections that identify all the key issues and topics to be covered. Don't forget to add relevant page numbers.

## Executive Summary

This section provides the reader with a brief synopsis of your photography business. Describe the business you intend to start and list the reasons you can make it successful. Include your goals, industry analysis, operations, inventory, and startup timetable. Limit this section to one or two pages by writing approximately one paragraph for each main section of the plan. Consider this your sales page by making the executive summary relevant, interesting, truthful, and engaging. Your goal is to make the reader want to continue reading the entire business plan.

## Mission Statement

As discussed earlier, this is an important element of the business plan. It sets the tone and direction this business will take and explains how the company's goals will be achieved. This section can also be expanded to include statements about your company's vision, values, unique services, and philosophy.

## Marketing Plan

Include an overview of the market and a description of your potential clients. Demonstrate that you've done your research. If you are a commercial photographer, use an online-based business directory to get a general idea of prospective business owners who could use your services.

Identify your competition and explain how you plan to corner the market. Discuss the advantages and drawbacks of your location, how you will deal with growth, and your strategy to promote your business through paid advertising (online and in the real world) as well as through other marketing and promotional efforts (including how you plan to use a website and social media).

FIGURE 5–2: **Business Plan Elements**

# Business Plan Elements

For example, if you plan to be a wedding photographer, talk about wedding expos where you plan to have a booth to showcase your work as well as strategic partnerships you have planned with local function halls, florists, bakeries, catering companies, wedding-dress makers, disc jockeys, wedding-band management companies, and tuxedo rental companies.

## Organizational Plan

In this section, confirm your legal structure—sole proprietorship, partnership, LLC, or corporation. Discuss your staffing needs and how you expect to meet them. Are you going to have employees who are full time, part time, or as needed? Are they family members, or will you go through a hiring process? Identify the consultants and advisors who will be assisting you and the certifications, licenses, permits, and other regulatory issues that will affect your company's operations.

Specify scheduled operating hours, including holidays. Provide short-term objectives for the immediate future as well as long-range goals for the next two, three, and five years.

## Management Plan

This is where you need to prove that you are up to the task of operating your own business. If you are homebased, chances are it will be a one-person operation. That's no problem as long as you are capable of successfully juggling multiple responsibilities.

Highlight your skills and business experience. If you have prior experience as a photographer—even as an amateur—be sure to describe it, along with any awards, credentials, accreditations, and/or other special acknowledgments you have earned.

## Financial Plan

This is where you show the source(s) of your startup capital and how you're going to use the money. Include information on real estate, fixtures, photography and business-related equipment, and insurance.

If you plan to seek investors or loans, include detailed financial statements, such as a balance sheet, profit-and-loss statement, break-even analysis, personal financial statements, and personal federal income tax returns.

Track your financial data and project for the upcoming year on a monthly basis to show what your business will do. Include a projected income statement for the second year with quarterly estimates and annual projections for three, four, and five years.

FIGURE 5–2: **Business Plan Elements,** continued

---

### Business Plan Elements

Follow the same formula for cash flow statements, along with worst-case income and cash flow statements to show what you'll do if your plan doesn't work. You may want to work with an accountant to help you compile this financial information.

**Summary**

Bring your plan together in this section. If you're trying to appeal to a funding source, use this section to reiterate the merits of your plan.

**Appendices**

Use this for supporting documents, such as your personal resume, and personal, business, and credit references. Attach a list of where your photographs have been published or exhibited. Include a studio design and layout. Perhaps showcase a small sampling of your photography work. Consider also adding marketing studies, sample advertising, copies of leases, and relevant licensing information. Any documentation that helps prove the validity of the information included earlier in the business plan should be added here.

---

FIGURE 5–2: **Business Plan Elements,** continued

Adobe Certification program for Photoshop and/or Lightroom (www.adobe.com/training/certification.html), for example.

When you think your business plan is complete, look at it with a fresh eye. Is it a true and honest representation of the facts? Is it realistic? Does it consider all the possible variables that could affect your operation? After you're satisfied, show the plan to two or three professional associates whose input you value and trust. Ask them to be brutally honest with their evaluation. You need to know if there are any glaring problems so you can correct them before they cost you time and money.

## Know Your Craft

It's assumed that if you are planning to launch a photography business that you already have photographic

**aha!**

Update your business plan every year. Choose an annual date when you will sit down with your plan, compare how closely your actual operation and results followed your forecasts, and decide if your plans for the coming year need adjusting. You will also need to take your financial forecasts out for another year, based on current and expected market conditions.

skills as well as familiarity with your photography equipment. You may even be a graduate of an accredited school with a degree in photojournalism or fine art. Regardless, continuing your photography-related education and training is essential if you want to succeed and stay ahead of the competition. For example, even if you've become highly proficient shooting with a digital SLR camera, you may discover the equipment upgrade involves a steep learning curve if you're about to upgrade to a full-frame mirrorless digital camera.

There are many opportunities for learning about photography from accredited colleges and companies that offer recognized certification programs both in-person and online. Following are some ways to obtain training that will help you fine-tune, enhance, or expand your photography knowledge and skill set.

## Go Back to School

Across America, you will find a number of accredited photography schools that offer training, certificates, and diplomas in photography and digital imaging. These schools enable students to get the necessary credentials to help launch a successful photography career. At the very least, they boost an individual's confidence as they acquire more knowledge in the field.

Many universities and colleges offer photography courses through their liberal and fine arts programs. You can find schools and courses that meet your requirements using a quick internet search. Be sure to obtain information about tuition and financial aid at the same time. Using your favorite internet search engine (Google, Yahoo, Bing, etc.), enter the search phrase "accredited photography schools" or "photography schools in [insert city or state]."

Typically, these programs offer a combination of classroom and hands-on experience while helping

**tip**

SCORE (www.score.org) is a free business mentoring program where successful current and retired business leaders volunteer their time to help up-and-coming business operators and entrepreneurs. If you don't have access to trusted people who can provide you with feedback and guidance as you launch your business, SCORE offers one-on-one mentoring programs and workshops that could be beneficial.

You can also enlist the aid of a mentor or counselor provided by the Small Business Development Center (a branch of the SBA). This, too, is a free service that will assist you with determining startup costs, finding loans and/or grants, and calculating realistic financial projections. It's a great solution for photographers thinking about going into business. For more information on where to find an office close to you, go to www.sba.gov.

## ▶ Financial Aid May Be Available

Discovering information about outside scholarships is relatively easy. Here are a few websites you should look into:

- ▶ *CollegeXpress* (www.collegexpress.com). Find scholarships, grants, and loans.
- ▶ *Coca-Cola Scholars Foundation* (www.coca-colascholarsfoundation.org). Scholarships are available to four-year college applicants as well as those attending technical schools and community colleges.
- ▶ *CollegeScholarships.com* (www.college-scholarships.com). Learn about scholarship opportunities, colleges, and online degrees.
- ▶ *Fastweb* (www.fastweb.com). Scholarships, financial aid, and college-related information is offered.
- ▶ *Scholarships.com* (www.scholarships.com). Find money for college.
- ▶ *SuperCollege.com* (www.supercollege.com). Look for loans and awards for high school, college, graduate, and adult students.

When you are applying for scholarships, grants, and loans, pay attention to deadlines. Once you've missed them, you've missed out. The earlier you apply, the better your chances of receiving financial aid.

students prepare their portfolios. They can also assist with internships and job placements in the "real world."

The cost of photography courses varies greatly; however, they will not be easy on the wallet. Financing is often available in the form of scholarships, grants, and loans. Some of the schools you apply to may also offer their own need- and merit-based scholarships.

## *Distance Learning (Online Education)*

Distance learning is one of the fastest-growing learning methods for education. This structure allows students to learn on their own time, in the comfort of their own home, at their own pace, while scheduling time around family commitments or work obligations. It does not require formal classroom attendance, which means that a student does not need to reside on campus or even nearby.

A student could live 500 miles away and still get a degree from an accredited college. Usually all coursework, examinations, reading, research, and writing assignments are done independently through an online study program.

The New York Institute of Photography (www.nyip.com) is the oldest and largest photography school in the world. It offers certification in various areas and year-round enrollment with a student body comprised mostly of adults in the 30- to 40-year-old age range.

Distance education classes can offer full-credit hours equivalent to those offered by a traditional course. It's also possible to sign up for one-time specialty courses that are relevant to your business.

## Workshops and Seminars

Informative workshops and seminars are continuously offered throughout the country. These are specialty one-, two-, or five-day courses that focus on a particular area in photography, such as lighting techniques or becoming a certified Adobe Photoshop professional.

You'll discover that camera manufacturers, including Nikon, Canon, and Leica, offer classes, workshops, and training programs to teach photographers about their latest equipment. Authorized camera sellers, including B&H Photo Video (www.bhphotovideo.com/find/Events.jsp) and Adorama (www.adorama.com/alc), also offer their own training programs.

## Reading Materials

For your reading enjoyment, your local library, retail bookseller, or favorite online retailer has a wealth of information on photography, business, marketing, and other relevant areas. Pick specific photography and/or business-related topics you want or need to learn about, then read at least two or three books that cover these topics in-depth.

## Online Learning Opportunities

Whatever photography or business-related topics you need to learn more about, video-based education is just a few keystrokes away. YouTube (www.youtube.com) offers thousands of free tutorial videos on photography-related topics, including specific camera models and how to use a variety of gear.

Other online education services offer many free and low-cost business and photography-related courses. Following are just a sampling:

> ► iTunes U (https://itunes.apple.com/us/app/itunes-u/id490217893)
> ► Udemy (www.udemy.com)
> ► Coursera (www.coursera.org)
> ► edX (www.edx.org)

When it comes to expanding your photography skills, Adobe (www.adobe.com/training/certification.html) offers a collection of online and video-based training programs taught by world-renowned photographers, as does KelbyOne (https://kelbyone.com).

# Become a Photography Assistant

Yet another option for improving your photography skill set while gaining hands-on experience is to find work as an assistant to an established and successful photographer. Working with and being able to learn from other photographers in a real-world setting will offer a realistic preview of what to expect when you're out on your own. Plus, by working with other photographers, this gives you exposure to various photography specialties. This experience can help you determine what specialties you enjoy.

As an assistant, your primary objective is not how much money you can make. Instead, focus on gaining knowledge and experience—even if you have to volunteer your time. Initially, you may not get many opportunities to stand behind the camera while on assignment. However, you will likely learn how to set up props and lighting, interact with customers, and successfully navigate your way around during an on-location shoot.

There is a real value in working with different photographers so that you can learn a variety of skills and techniques. It also gives you the opportunity to observe how other business models work.

Just as you would with any employer, do your homework and research the photographers you are considering working with. This will help you to assess their needs and be sure they are ethical and trustworthy individuals who will not take advantage of you.

Once you have a list of photographers you would like to contact, approach them in a professional manner by sending them your resume and a note expressing your interest in working with them. You can use the "Contact Us" function on their website or message them using LinkedIn.

Also, based on the photography specialty you're considering, find a professional association or organization that caters to that niche and join it. Be sure to attend local chapter meetings so you can meet, interact with, and potentially learn from other members.

Some of the professional associations/organizations you might consider joining include:

▶ American Society of Media Photographers (www.asmp.org)

▶ Professional Photographers of America (www.ppa.com)

▶ American Photographic Artists (https://apanational.org/events/upcoming)

▶ National Press Photographers Association (https://nppa.org)

▶ Society of International Fashion & Glamour Photographers (www.sifgp.com)

▶ Women in Photography International (www.womeninphotography.org)

▶ Wedding & Portrait Photography International (www.wppiexpo.com)

▶ Wedding Photojournalist Association (www.wpja.com)

▶ American Society of Picture Professionals (http://aspp.com)

# Shoot for Accessibility: Choosing Your Location

One of the main attractions of starting a photography business is that you can start relatively small as a solopreneur. Yes, you'll need to invest a lot of money in camera equipment, lenses, and related gear, but the costs associated with establishing and operating the actual business are relatively low. Whether you operate from the comfort of your home or run your business from a commercial location, you need a place to store your equipment. You'll also need the right supplies to set up shop.

The ideal location for your photography business depends on the type of services you are going to provide, how much equipment and cash you have to start with, and what your goals are. Basically, your two choices are homebased or a commercial location. If you opt for the latter, you'll have some additional choices to make that will be discussed later in this chapter.

Many photographers start as a homebased operation with no desire to change that status since it offers convenience and flexibility as well as the least amount of financial outlay. Others start at home, but eventually are faced with the need to expand their operation into a bigger space, especially if they want to do portraiture with backgrounds (which take up a ton of space). Still others set up their studio in a commercial location at the onset or plan to do so as soon as they have sufficient revenue. Keep in mind, with adequate planning, a photography business can be operated from almost any location—it all depends on your needs.

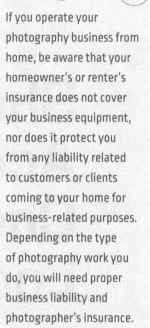

**warning**

If you operate your photography business from home, be aware that your homeowner's or renter's insurance does not cover your business equipment, nor does it protect you from any liability related to customers or clients coming to your home for business-related purposes. Depending on the type of photography work you do, you will need proper business liability and photographer's insurance. You can read more about insurance in Chapter 7.

When deciding where to operate from, think about what you must have to operate your business, what you'd like to have, what you absolutely won't tolerate, and how much you're able to pay. Give this process the time it deserves by listing these needs and desires on paper. A poor location choice can be an expensive mistake that is difficult and costly to remedy. Let's take a look at the most common options for setting up shop.

## Home Sweet Studio

One of the key benefits of a homebased business is that it significantly reduces the amount of startup and initial operating capital you'll need. But there's more to consider than simply the upfront cash. You need to be conveniently located so your clients can find you, if necessary, and so you can get to them—or to other places you need to go—without spending an excessive amount of travel time.

If your location works, consider your home from a capacity perspective. Do you have a separate room available for your business, or will you have to do paperwork on a corner of the dining room table? You will find it helpful to separate your work area from the rest of the house so you can have privacy when you're working and can get away from "the office" when you're not. Do you have adequate storage for equipment and supplies? Many photographers who work from home say that having enough (climate-controlled) storage space is one of their biggest challenges.

The ideal situation for the homebased photographer is to set aside a room (or rooms) exclusively for your business use. If you can't, do the best you can with the resources and space you have. Just remember that to take the home office deduction on your taxes, the IRS requires that you have at least one room that is dedicated solely to your business. If you're only using part of a room or if your office doubles as a den or guest room, a home office deduction may not survive an IRS audit. Discuss this with your accountant before proceeding. You can, of course, deduct all other allowable business expenses.

**warning**

If you live in a residential area that is not zoned for commercial purposes relating to customers coming and going from the location, a homebased business may not be viable. You'll need to contact local government, your homeowner's association, or your landlord to determine what's permissible where you live.

So, what can you deduct in a homebased business? You can deduct directly related expenses, which are those that benefit only the business part of your home, and a portion of indirect expenses, which are the costs involved in keeping up and running your entire home. For example, your office furniture, computer(s), and photography equipment are fully deductible as directly related expenses.

In the area of indirect expenses, you may deduct a portion of your household utilities and services (electric, gas, water, sewage, trash collection, etc.) based on the percentage of use for business purposes. This also includes your internet service, especially if you regularly communicate with customers via email, operate a company website, or use cloud-based services to manage, backup, and archive your digital photo library.

Other examples of indirect expenses include real estate taxes, deductible mortgage interest, casualty losses, rent, insurance, repairs, security systems, and depreciation. You can also deduct other expenses—camera equipment, related photography gear, inventory, storage, supplies, automobile, marketing, etc.—that are legitimate costs associated with doing business. All that said, keep in mind that the Tax Cuts and

**tip**

Even though you're homebased, take care that you present yourself as a serious businessperson. If clients visit your home, your office should reflect your professionalism. Also, any other areas of your home that clients may see should be neat, orderly, and create a positive impression.

Jobs Act (TCJA) that went into effect in 2018 may change how some of these deductions can impact your business's bottom line. For the latest on how the new tax code affects small-business owners, visit www.irs.gov/tax-reform. You can also pick up Mark Kohler's *Tax and Legal Playbook, Second Edition* (Entrepreneur Press, 2019) to get his take on the best ways to maximize your business deductions.

If converting a den or spare bedroom into an office and work area is not possible or if your operation requires a large amount of space, you may want to consider transforming the basement or garage into a suitable work area. Only do this if the basement or garage offers a clean, dry, climate-controlled, and secure space for your equipment.

## Choosing a Commercial Location

If you do not have adequate space at home, or if you are unable to set up your business because of zoning or other restrictions, you will need to buy or lease office and/or studio space. Studios can be in almost any type of neighborhood or building, including industrial areas, which generally cost less than commercial or retail space. Just make sure you choose a location that offers clients ample parking and that they'll feel safe visiting.

Starting in a commercial location requires more initial cash than starting from home, but the additional business you attract will hopefully offset the expense. When looking at commercial locations, your choice should be guided largely by the specific services you want to provide and the market you plan to reach.

Before investing in a commercial facility, be sure the surrounding market is favorable for the studio you envision and the location is consistent with your style and image. Consider these questions:

**aha!**

You can often find fully equipped, shared photography studio spaces to rent or lease in larger, metropolitan cities. These tend to include plenty of background options, professional lighting setups, and sometimes even assistants.

▶ Will your clients be comfortable coming there?

▶ Is the facility accessible to people with disabilities?

▶ If you're on a busy street, how easy is it for cars to get in and out of the parking lot?

▶ If you're in a multitenant building, are there specific days and hours of service and access?

▶ Are the heating and cooling systems left on or turned off at night and on weekends?

▶ If you don't have your own entrance, are there periods when the exterior doors are locked, and if so, will you have keys?

These are just a few questions to ponder as you explore potential spaces, but take into consideration your own personal needs and wants as well so you can narrow the list of possible spaces.

## Commercial Leases

If this is your first venture into leasing property, you may initially find yourself a bit overwhelmed. Lease documents are often cumbersome, wordy, and hard to understand. To make matters worse, they are usually written to the landlord's benefit. Most leases, however, are negotiable.

Follow a few simple guidelines as you negotiate a lease. First, you need to understand what the lease documents say. If you are having trouble deciphering the lingo, talk to a Realtor or hire an attorney. Second, you need to know exactly what you want out of this transaction before going to the table. A long, drawn-out negotiation process could kill a deal. Third, you need to be reasonable with your demands. You will be surprised at what you can get if you ask nicely. The initial lease is just a starting point. Following are the lease items that are subject to negotiation:

▶ Start of rent and lease amount (include antici-pated increases)

▶ Length of lease

▶ Termination clause

▶ Configuration of the physical space

▶ Tenant improvements

▶ Tenant's rights and exposures

▶ Common area maintenance costs

▶ Construction allowance (use if you need to do a substantial amount of work to prepare the space for occupancy)

▶ Subleases and assignments (important if you are going to share space or need to get out of the lease early)

**warning** ⚠

Once you sign a 12-month lease, for example, you are obligated to pay the monthly lease/rent payments for the full period, regardless of whether or not your business generates a profit or if it goes belly up. Do not sign a lease that you can't afford if your income does not live up to projections.

Before you sign a lease, make sure you have considered everything. How many rent increases have there been during the past three years? How old is the roof? Find out if there are any anticipated repairs coming up in the near future. The more you know, the less risk you will have.

## Sharing Space

Not crazy about leasing commercial space but can't work out of your home? Another option to consider is sharing a studio with one or two other photographers. Naturally, this type of arrangement has its own pros and cons. The biggest advantage is reducing your rent. This often helps you project the image of a professional operation at a more affordable cost. It's essentially the same as having a roommate, but you'll need to work out a written agreement to make sure everyone has a clear understanding of what's expected from each party. You should address the following:

▶ What days and times will each photographer have use of the studio?

▶ Will you share an assistant or have your own employees?

▶ Will you share some of the equipment?

**tip**

Many cities have large, spacious photography studios available to rent for special assignments. Although his own studio is adequate for most jobs, Michael Weschler said he sometimes needs something more deluxe for bigger productions. He explains, "There may be a celebrity or advertising shoot where we need a kitchen or more square footage to accommodate the props, so I'll end up renting another studio."

## ▶ What's Your Sign?

Nothing shouts the news that you are open for business louder than an effective, well-designed sign. A homebased operation may not be permitted to have a business sign, so check with your local zoning board before having one made. But if you're in a commercial location, you'll definitely want to have a clear, easy-to-see sign so clients can find you.

Keep in mind that 1-inch letters are easily seen 10 feet away, 2-inch letters can be seen at 20 feet, and so on. Don't create a sign with letters so small that your clients can't easily read them. Also keep the font simple; fancy lettering with flourishes may be difficult to decipher. You can read more about creating a logo in Chapter 7.

▶ How will maintenance and cleaning responsibilities be divvied up? (A better alternative may be to outsource those duties.)

▶ What type of termination clause will you have in the event one of you splits before the end of the lease?

**aha!**

When it comes to creating all sorts of signage and tradeshow displays, one full-service and affordable company you might want to work with is Post-Up Stand (www.postupstand.com). In addition to manufacturing and printing signage and tradeshow booths, the company has a talented in-house design team.

Michael Weschler shares a studio in New York City with another photographer, which allows him to have a place to land between location shoots. "I shoot mostly on location, so I don't need a full-time studio," he says. "It's a co-op arrangement, so we're not there at the same time. Whatever day or week I'm scheduled for, then the studio is mine to use."

As important as it is to have an eye-catching sign at your location, promoting your business online is an absolute must. You'll need to establish a website for your photography business but also obtain business listings on online-based services such as Yelp, Google Maps, and Apple Maps.

For details on how to use these online services to promote your location-based business, visit their websites:

▶ Apple Maps (https://mapsconnect.apple.com)

▶ Google (www.google.com/business)

▶ Yelp (https://biz.yelp.com/support/claiming)

Once your business has a listing on these and other services, make sure you maintain those listings with up-to-date contact, location, and hours of operation information. Also understand that people will publish ratings and reviews for your business online. Maintaining an average five-star rating on these services will help boost your business, but anything lower than a four-star average rating will be detrimental to your business.

## Should You Franchise?

Franchising can be a great way to start a new business because even though you are in business for yourself, you're not alone. You can start your new venture with a proven working model, an enthusiastic team of go-getters, and comprehensive hands-on training. Believe it or not, the photography industry has a good amount of franchises that you can buy into if you want the backing of an established brand. Some of the more active photography franchise brands include:

- ▶ TSS Photography (https://tssphotography.com). School, sports, and event photography.
- ▶ Lil' Angels Photography (http://lilangelsphoto.com). Children and family portraiture.
- ▶ PortraitEFX Photography (https://portraitefx.com). School, church, sports, and special event photography.
- ▶ Spoiled Rotten Photography (https://spoiledrottenphotography.com). Children's portraiture and event photography.

## How Franchising Works

In a nutshell, the franchisor lends their trademark or trade name and business model to the franchisee, who pays a royalty and often an initial fee for the right to do business under the franchisor's name and system. The contract binding the two parties is the franchise, but that term is also used to describe the business the franchisee operates.

The best part for the franchisee is the franchisor has already worked the kinks out of the system and is available to help franchisees when new challenges arise. According to the SBA, most independent, small-business startups fail from lack of management skills. This is less likely to happen with a franchised business because your franchisor is there to guide you through the maze of business ownership.

Typically, you think of fast food and restaurants when you think of franchising, but virtually every business form has the potential to be franchised.

## The Cons

While there are many potential benefits to owning a franchise (security, training, and marketing power), there are some drawbacks. Perhaps the most significant is the cost. The initial franchise fee can run anywhere from a few thousand to several hundred thousand dollars. Then, you have continuing royalty payments to the franchisor based on the weekly or monthly gross income of your business. Additional expenses may include promotional and advertising fees, operating licenses and permits, insurance, and other costs of running a business.

Another big drawback is that you have to give up some of your independence. Each franchise is different in how firm conditions and requirements are; however, you will be bound by the contract to follow and implement the rules and procedures established by the franchisor. For example, if you neglect to pay your royalty fees or misbehave by not meeting performance standards, your franchise could be terminated and you could lose your investment. So, if you like to make your own decisions and "do your own thing," a franchise may not be right for you.

You also have no control over how the franchisor operates, and the corporate office can make decisions that you do not agree with or reduce your profitability. That's why it's so important to thoroughly research a franchise; you want to see a positive operational pattern before making a commitment. If a particular franchise piques your interest, before doing anything, make direct contact with a handful of existing franchise owners and learn about their firsthand experiences.

Much of the information you'll need about a franchise is provided in the form of a document known as the UFOC, or Uniform Franchise Offering Circular. Under Federal Trade Commission (FTC) rules, you must receive this document at least ten business days before you are asked to sign any contract or pay any money to the franchisor.

To learn more about franchising opportunities for photography-related businesses, check out these online resources:

▶ Entrepreneur (www.entrepreneur.com/franchises/category/svcphoto)
▶ Franchise Direct (www.franchisedirect.com)
▶ Franchise Rankings (www.franchiserankings.com/reviews-and-ratings-of-best-photography-franchises)

## Buying an Existing Business

An alternative to a franchise or to starting your own business is to take over an existing studio or established photography business from a photographer who is retiring or going out of business. Often, this type of business can be purchased lock, stock, and barrel, including photography and office equipment, supplies, backdrops, props, the space itself, and most important, a client base. While this may seem like a simple and logical shortcut for anyone starting a new photography business, you should approach this option with caution.

One of the disadvantages of buying a previously owned business is that not only do you get the company's assets, but you also assume its liabilities. For example, what if the building is in serious disrepair or the owner hasn't paid taxes in the last five years? Another concern is losing clientele when the owner leaves. Although the business name may still be the same, their relationship is with the previous owner, not you. The best-case scenario would be for the owner to hang around for a while in an advisory capacity to help everyone feel more comfortable with the transition.

You'll find a variety of businesses for sale advertised in trade publications, local newspapers, on the internet, and by working with a reputable business broker. Before making a final decision, make sure you have done all your homework by finding out the following details:

**tip**

If you buy an existing business, include a noncompete clause in your terms of sale. Your new business won't be worth much if the seller opens a competing operation down the street a few weeks after you take over the old company.

- ► Find out why the business is for sale. Don't accept what the current owner says at face value; do some research to make an independent confirmation.
- ► Examine the business's financial records for the previous three years and for the current year-to-date. Compare tax records with the owner's claims of revenue and profits.
- ► Spend time (days or weeks) observing the operation. For example, if you're looking at a wedding photography business, tag along to a couple of the events.
- ► Check what equipment and supplies will be transferred to the new owner. What is the equipment's condition, and will it suit your needs? How much will you need to invest in upgrading your photography equipment and gear to be competitive?
- ► Determine the cost of remodeling if the studio's current setup is not conducive to your future plans.
- ► Speak with current clients. Are they satisfied with the service? Are they willing to give a new owner a chance? Ask for their input, both positive and negative, and ask what you can do to improve the operation. Remember, even though sales volume and cash flow may be a primary reason for buying an existing business, customers are under no obligation to stay with you when you take over.
- ► Find out what the leasing arrangements are with the landlord. Is there a mortgage or long-term lease that needs to be assumed?

Finally, consider hiring someone skilled in business acquisitions to assist you in negotiating the sale price and terms of the deal. Regardless of whether you choose to buy an existing business, start from scratch, or purchase a franchise, having a business acquisitions expert, CPA, or attorney involved can help you avoid legal issues down the road.

# Business Structure: A Blueprint for Success

There's a lot to do when you start your photography business. This chapter addresses some important issues and helps you map out a blueprint for success as you get set up.

## A Name to Remember

One of your best marketing tools is the name of your business. A well-chosen name—whether it's your own or a fictitious one—can work hard for you. An ineffective name means you have to work much harder at marketing your company.

Many photographers use their own name for their business. Some examples include: "John Doe Photography," "John Doe Portrait Studio," "Jane Doe Wedding & Event Photography," or "Portrait Photography by John Doe." This option has several benefits. One is you don't have to trademark your name because it's already yours. Using your own name not only improves your personal credibility as your photography business grows, but it will build prestige within the community. It won't take long for people to recognize your name and associate it with your business.

On the flip side, you don't want to stunt the growth of your business by its namesake. The name, "Jane Doe Wedding Photography" unquestionably states the nature of this business—shooting weddings; however, if Jane Doe wants to expand her services to include parties, bar mitzvahs, and corporate events, the name would no longer be effective. Use Figure 7–1, Business Name Worksheet, on page 71 to help you brainstorm potential company names.

## Getting Creative

Ideally, your business name should clearly identify what you do. If it's too obscure or cryptic, people will have no idea what your business does. Make the name short, catchy, and memorable—but not cute. There's a fine line between clever and cute. Clever is captivating; cute is comical. Comical is unprofessional. Don't be cute. Your company name should also be easy to pronounce and spell. People who can't say your business name may use your services, but they won't be able to tell anyone else about you or remember the name of your business.

Though naming your company is without a doubt a creative process, it helps to take a systematic approach. Once you've decided on a name, or perhaps two or three possibilities, check to see if any other business has a similar name. Two different companies with similar names will confuse potential customers.

## Make It Legal

After deciding on a company name, check to make sure it's legally available. How you do this depends on what legal

**tip**

Look on the internet to see if your name is already in use. This can easily be done through a "WHOIS" database of a domain registrar, such as GoDaddy (www.godaddy.com). If someone is already using your company's name as a domain name, you can select one of the alternate names recommended by the domain registrar, consider a different name, or use the free domain suggestion tool at NameTumbler (www.nametumbler.com).

## Business Name Worksheet

List three (or more) variations using your own name for your business:

1. _____

2. _____

3. _____

List three business name ideas associated with your specialty or niche as a photographer (e.g., weddings, commercial, fine art):

1. _____

2. _____

3. _____

List three business name ideas associated with your geographical area. You can use the name of your town, county, or state.

1. _____

2. _____

3. _____

Narrow down your name options to your top one or two choices by taking the following steps:

- ▶ Write it down to see how it looks.

- ▶ Say it aloud to hear how it sounds.

- ▶ Check the first initials of each word to make sure the acronym isn't something inappropriate.

- ▶ Run it by family and friends to see if they are as enthusiastic as you are.

- ▶ Do an internet search to see if someone else is using the same or a similar name.

- ▶ Call the county clerk or secretary of state's office to arrange to file it.

FIGURE 7–1: **Business Name Worksheet**

structure you choose, which is discussed in the next section. In the meantime, call your local business licensing agency to get more information on registering a fictitious name. If you are a sole proprietor or corporation using the name of the owner(s), you probably will not be required to register it; however, you may still want to consider it so no one else can use that name.

Also, check to see if the name conflicts with any that are listed on your state or county's trademark register. Your state's department of commerce can help you or direct you to the correct agency. You should also check with the trademark register maintained by the U.S. Patent and Trademark Office (PTO).

Once the name you've chosen passes these tests (and you now can register a .com website URL for it), you need to protect it by registering it with the appropriate state agency; again, your state's department of commerce can help you. If you anticipate doing business nationally, you should also register the name with the PTO.

## Register Your Domain ASAP

After choosing a business name, visit a domain registrar, such as GoDaddy.com, Google Domains (https://domains.google), or Name.com (www.name.com), and register the website URL for that company name. Here are some guidelines for choosing a website URL for your business:

▶ Make sure the website name is easy to spell and remember.

▶ The website URL should end with ".com." While other domain name extensions are available, such as .photo, .photography, .biz, and .info, the majority of web surfers automatically type ".com" when entering a domain name into their web browser. If you can't obtain the ".com" domain extension for your selected business name, choose an alternate URL that still reflects your business name. For example, if www.janedoephotography.com is taken, perhaps www.janedoephoto.com would work.

▶ Make sure your domain name does not infringe on someone else's trademark or copyright.

▶ Figure out the top misspellings or typos related to your business name and URL, then register those domain names as well. Set it up so the misspelled versions of the URLs direct to your main website. For example, www.JasonRichPhotography.com and www.JaysonRichPhotgography.com should bring web surfers to the same websites . . . your website.

▶ At the same time you acquire the .com website URL, use the same domain to set up your email accounts, such as jason@jasonrichphotography.com and info@jasonrichphotography.com.

There is an annual fee associated with registering each domain name. It's typically under $20 per year for a .com URL. (Domain names ending in other extensions may be priced higher.) However, you can often save money by prepaying your domain registration fees for multiple years upfront.

To avoid being bombarded with telemarketing calls from overseas-based website designers, add the privacy option when registering your domain name(s). Remember, at the same time you register your domain name, obtain email accounts using the same domain name.

# Build Your Brand with a Logo

Once you've chosen a name for your photography business, get a company logo designed. You'll use this logo to promote your company on your website, letterhead, business cards, advertising, and social media as well as a watermark on images included in your portfolio.

A company called Photologo (https://photologo.co) specializes is designing custom logos for photographers and photography businesses for as little as $39.99. If you pay a rush fee, you can have a logo designed in as little as 24 or 48 hours.

Photologo also sells specialized, easy-to-use, PC and Mac software that makes watermarking your digital images (using your logo) extremely fast and easy. You can control the size, position, transparency, and color of your watermark.

Showcasing a professional logo instantly boosts the credibility of your business and helps you develop a professional reputation. It also helps build brand recognition and will help differentiate your business from the competition.

Beyond using Photologo, you can quickly find graphic artists to design a company logo for you using a service like Upwork (www.upwork.com), Freelancer.com (www.freelancer.com), or Toptal (www.toptal.com/designers/graphic). Canva.com (www.canva.com) is another good resource for securing an original logo and finding help developing a visual brand for your photography business

**aha!**

If you'll be using an original logo to promote your business on a national or international level, for example, it might make sense to obtain a registered trademark for it. For information on how to do this and determine if it's necessary based on the scope of your work, visit the website for the U.S. Patent and Trademark Office. For help filing a trademark, use a fee-based, online service, such as LegalZoom (www.legalzoom.com).

and for you as a photographer. There, you can set up a free account and play around with all sorts of designs and order products featuring your logo.

## Structure It Legally

You need to give some thought to your company's legal structure and register it accordingly with your city, state, and federal governments, as required by law. Your choice can affect your financial liability, the amount of taxes you pay, and the degree of control you have over the company. It can also have an impact on your ability to raise money, attract investors, and later sell the business.

If you're starting the business by yourself, you'll be the one making all the decisions. However, if other people are involved, you need to consider the issue of asset protection and limiting your financial liability in the event things don't go well.

Legal business structures include:

▶ *Sole proprietorship.* Many homebased entrepreneurs prefer to be classified as sole proprietors—at least initially. It's not unusual for a business owner to change that status later to include a partner or to incorporate as the business grows. The beauty of sole proprietorship is its simplicity. There's not a lot to do in the way of paperwork and filing fees. But the disadvantage of being a sole proprietor is that if anything goes wrong (e.g., you are sued or default on a loan), creditors can go after your personal assets.

▶ *Partnership.* When two or more people go into business together, a partnership is formed. This type of arrangement can come in handy if you want to share a studio or split hefty equipment costs. Just make sure you have a well-written agreement in place. A partnership works like a sole proprietorship, except the partners share in the profits, expenses, and liabilities of the business.

▶ *Limited liability company (LLC).* This type of structure has a lot of the same elements as a partnership or corporation, but it can reduce the partners' or shareholders' potential liability. From a legal and tax standpoint, there's a bit more involved than operating a sole proprietorship or partnership.

**tip** ⓘ

When it comes to filing tax returns, the easiest option is to use a sole proprietorship. Income and losses from your business are filed as part of your personal income tax returns. Be sure to discuss your options and tax liabilities with an accountant and/or business lawyer before making any decisions.

▶ *Incorporation.* Typically, a corporation is comprised of shareholders who elect a director, who nominates officers, who then hire employees to manage and operate the company. But it's entirely possible for a corporation to have only one shareholder and to essentially function as a sole proprietorship. The biggest advantage of forming a corporation is in the area of asset protection—making sure the assets you don't want to put into the business don't stand liable for the debt of the business. A corporation becomes its own legal entity. You need to file separate tax returns for it and file other paperwork with the state and federal government on a regular basis. For help creating a corporation, contact a business lawyer or accountant, or use an independent, online-based service such as LegalZoom.com.

Choose an option that works best for you and offers the best protection. Consider what you want to do now and where you expect to take your company. Choose the form that is most appropriate for your needs.

Finally, remember that your choice of legal structure is not an irreversible decision; although if you're going to make a switch, it's easier to go from the simpler forms to the more sophisticated ones than the other way around. The typical pattern is to start as a sole proprietorship and move up to a corporation as the business grows. However, if you think you need the asset protection of a corporation from the beginning, that is how you should start out.

If there's any chance of getting sued by a customer or client for any type of liability or injury, maintaining a corporation offers the most personal protection from a legal and financial standpoint. Of course, you also need to start with the right types of business insurance.

## Licenses and Permits

Most cities, counties, and/or states require business owners to obtain licenses and permits to comply with local regulations. While you're still in the planning stages, check with your local planning and zoning department, or city/county/state business license department to find out what licenses and permits you will need for your photography business, and in what order you need to obtain them.

You may need one, some, or all of the following:

▶ *Occupational license or permit.* This is typically required by the city (or county, if you are not within an incorporated city) for just about every business operating within its jurisdiction. License fees are essentially a tax, and the rates vary widely based on the location and type of business. As part of the application process, the licensing bureau will check to make sure there are no zoning restrictions prohibiting you from operating in your location.

▶ *Fire department permit.* If your business is open to the public or in a commercial location, you may be required to have a permit from the local fire department.

▶ *Sign permit.* Many cities and suburbs have sign ordinances that restrict the size, location, and sometimes the lighting or type of sign you can use in front of your business. Landlords may also impose their own restrictions. Most residential areas forbid signs altogether. Before you get too artistic, check regulations and secure the written approval of your landlord (if applicable) to avoid costly mistakes.

▶ *State licenses.* Many states require people engaged in certain occupations to hold licenses or occupational permits. This would also include a license for sales and use taxes, which most states require for anyone (including photographers) engaged in the sale of products and services to clients. Check with your state's department of revenue.

▶ *Federal licenses.* It's rare, but sometimes federal licensing is required. This is really more for a business that is government regulated. However, if you are conducting business across state lines or running ads in another state, contact the FTC. Then consult with an attorney who can guide you through the application process.

**warning**

Find out what type of licenses and permits are required for your business while you're still in the planning stage. You may find out that you can't legally operate the business you're envisioning from a particular location, so give yourself time to make adjustments to your strategy before you've spent a lot of time and money trying to move in an impossible direction.

## Covering Your Assets

In the absence of a crystal ball, you can't foresee every hazard lurking around the corner that might potentially jeopardize your livelihood. However, you can take the necessary steps to protect yourself and your business with adequate insurance. Sit down with an insurance agent who is familiar with your type of business, analyze your potential risks and exposures, then purchase appropriate and sufficient coverage. Focus on both liability insurance for your business as well as insurance that will cover your camera equipment and gear against loss, theft, or damage. Some common types of business insurance include:

## ▶ Laying the Foundation

Deciding what type of business structure you need can sometimes be confusing and overwhelming. Think about the following questions as you ponder these important decisions:

▶ How many owners does your business have? If more than one, what are their roles and will they have equal participation?

▶ Do you want to be the main or only decision maker?

▶ How concerned are you about asset protection or tax consequences?

▶ Is cost a factor in determining your business structure? If so, understand you can always change the structure as your business grows.

▶ How much paperwork can you realistically handle? Some structures involve more administrative work than others.

▶ Will employees be allowed to participate and become part owners in the business?

▶ Do you want your investors to be shareholders in the business? If so, do you still want to maintain control or share those duties?

Revisit these questions at least once a year. As your business grows, its needs will change and so will some of the structural decisions you previously made.

▶ *Property insurance.* This type of policy covers the building and contents (including some equipment) in the event of damage, theft, or loss.

▶ *Contents insurance.* If you are leasing studio space, contents insurance will reimburse you in the event of destruction, damage, or theft.

▶ *General liability insurance.* This will protect you and your business from liability in the event someone—customer or an employee—sues you for personal injuries or property damage. Let's say your assistant trips over a tungsten light and burns their leg. If they decide to sue you for loss of wages and punitive damages, the cost of defending yourself could be prohibitive. That's why this type of insurance is so important. It also offers coverage if you accidentally injure a customer or royally screw up a job and get sued as a result.

▶ *Umbrella policy.* This basically covers your other insurance policies, like property, casualty, and general liability, in case they exceed their limits when a claim is filed.

▶ *Business interruption insurance.* This protects you from loss of revenue in the event of property damage or loss. For example, if you were unable to conduct business because a storm caused extensive damage to your studio, you would be reimbursed for rents, taxes, and income that would have been earned during the down time.

▶ *Disability and health insurance.* Let's face it, life happens. No matter how young or healthy you are, there is always the possibility you may be thrown a curve ball that could cause a serious setback. There are numerous kinds of health and disability policies that can be customized to fit your lifestyle and budget if you should ever become sick, injured, or disabled.

▶ *Life insurance.* What if life really zaps you? Will your untimely demise create a financial hardship for loved ones? Tough things to think about, but it pays to be prepared for the unexpected.

Unfortunately, there is not a one-plan-fits-all insurance policy. A qualified insurance agent can help you anticipate unforeseen events, evaluate your risks, and determine which ones you need to insure against. Using an internet search engine, do a search for "photographer's insurance" to learn about types of policies that offer protection for yourself, your equipment, and your clients based on the type(s) of photography work you plan to do.

> **tip**
>
> Find out from your insurance agent what documentation the insurance company requires in the event of a claim—especially for inventory and equipment. This way, you will be sure to maintain accurate records and have them available if you need to file a claim report. Keep detailed records and receipts for all your costly camera equipment and related gear. Make sure you record serial numbers related to your camera and other applicable equipment. It's also a good idea to have photos of your equipment that you can present to an insurance adjuster if anything needs to be replaced.

## People You Should Know

As a business owner, you may be the boss, but you can't be expected to know everything. There are going to be times and situations when you'll need to turn to other professionals for information and assistance. Now is the time to establish relationships with these professionals—before you get into a crisis situation.

To look for a professional service provider, ask friends and associates for recommendations. You might also check with your local chamber of commerce, trade association, or LinkedIn contacts for referrals.

Find people who understand your industry and specific business and who appear eager to work with you. Keep in mind that you are going to have a personal relationship with these people, so it's important that you feel at ease with them. If you hit a snag, they will be the ones who will help to bail you out.

The professional service providers you're likely to need include:

▶ *Accountant.* Whether directly or indirectly, your accountant will most likely have the greatest impact on the success or failure of your business. A good accountant will always be aware of the ever-changing tax laws and how they apply to your business. They can counsel you on tax issues if you are forming a corporation as well as advise what types of business deductions you are eligible for. Your accountant can assist in charting future actions based on past performance, help you organize financial records, and advise you on your overall financial strategy with matters related to your business goals. A good accountant will also serve as a tax advisor, making sure you are in compliance with all applicable regulations and that you don't overpay any taxes. Make sure your accountant supports the bookkeeping software you choose to manage your company's finances. Intuit's QuickBooks (www.quickbooks.com), for example, is software used by many small businesses and entrepreneurs.

▶ *Attorney.* Look for a lawyer who practices in the area of business law, has a good reputation, and values your patronage. Interview several attorneys and choose one with whom you feel comfortable. There is usually no charge for an initial consultation, but make sure to clarify this before making an appointment. Good attorneys don't come cheap, so you'll also want to establish the fee schedule ahead of time and get your agreement in writing. Once you have retained an attorney, let them review all contracts, leases, letters of intent, and other legal documents before you sign them. They can also help you collect bad debts and establish personnel policies and procedures. Whenever you are unsure of the legal ramifications of any situation, call your attorney immediately.

▶ *Insurance agent.* A good independent insurance agent can assist you with all aspects of your business insurance from general liability to workers' compensation. Look for an agent who works with a wide range of insurers and understands your particular business. There are many differ-

**warning**

Not all attorneys are created equal, and you may need more than one. For example, the lawyer who can best guide you in contract negotiations may not be the most effective counsel when it comes to copyright issues. Ask about areas of expertise and specialization before retaining a lawyer.

ent types of coverage. Your agent should be willing to discuss the various details, while helping you determine the most appropriate coverage. They should also help you understand the degree of risk you are taking and what remedies are available to minimize risks. Even more important, your agent should assist with expediting any claims that may arise.

► *Banker.* In addition to a business bank account, you should have a good relationship with a local banker. The bank you've always done your personal banking with may not necessarily be the best bank for your business. Talk to several bankers before deciding where you'll handle the finances for your business. Maintain your relationship with your banker by reviewing your accounts periodically and making sure the services you use are the most appropriate ones for your current situation. Ask for advice if you have financial questions or problems. When you need a loan or a bank reference to provide to creditors, the relationship you've established will work in your favor.

► *Other experts.* As your business grows, you may need to seek the services of other types of professionals. A business consultant can help you evaluate your business plan, a marketing consultant can assist you with marketing strategies, and a human resources consultant can teach you how to avoid costly mistakes when you are ready to hire employees. There is also the computer expert who can help you maintain, troubleshoot, and upgrade your computers and

**aha!**

If you plan to do any online-based advertising or marketing, hiring an independent, skilled specialist who knows how to use services like Google Ads and various social media advertising platforms on Facebook, Twitter, Instagram, or Pinterest, for example, can help you get the most out of your ad spending while carefully targeting your intended audience.

Don't just rely on sales representatives who work directly for the online service you choose to advertise with. These people want you to spend the most money possible, typically won't truly understand your business and its goals, and often don't have your company's best interests in mind when making suggestions. You can find online advertising specialists by doing a search online. Some companies that offer website design and hosting services for photographers also offer fee-based tools and resources to help you advertise and promote your business.

related technologies as needed, while a web designer can develop a professional-looking online presence for your business.

No matter how good you are at what you do, chances are you can't do it all—and you shouldn't—so find ways to network and get in touch with professionals who can help make your business a success.

# Business Equipment for the Photographer

Before opening for business, you'll need to gather all the appropriate equipment. You already read about determining an initial budget for equipment in Chapter 4, but now, let's dive deeper into the list of what you'll need to take high-quality photos and to run the business side of your studio. This list of must-have equipment falls into five distinct categories:

1. *Camera equipment and related gear.* This includes everything from your camera(s) to an assortment of lenses, flashes, memory cards, tripods, carrying cases, and batteries.

2. *Studio equipment.* This covers the lighting, backdrops, props, set pieces, and other essentials needed to take portraits and other types of photos in an indoor studio setting.

3. *Computer equipment and related technology.* You'll need desktop and laptop computers, a laser printer, photo printer, wireless router, large monitor(s), along with specialized photography software (such as Photoshop, Lightroom, PortraitPro), business applications (that include word processing, presentation, and spreadsheet programs), and bookkeeping software. If you'll be accepting credit and debit card payments from customers and clients, you'll also need appropriate software and equipment for that, especially if you plan to take payment in the field.

4. *Office equipment.* This includes everything from file cabinets, desks, and telephone(s) to a photocopy machine and office supplies.

5. *Company branding, sales, and marketing tools.* Don't forget your business cards, signage, letterhead, brochures, invoices, and other materials that will feature your logo, slogan, contact information, and sales information.

You don't need every single piece of equipment listed in this chapter to get started, but at least you have some things to consider based on your goals and growth strategy.

## The Photographer's Case

What kind of photography equipment do you need to succeed? There are too many variables to provide you with clear-cut suggestions. Your needs will largely be dependent on what type of photography you do, where you'll be shooting, and your budget. If you're on a tight budget but still need to invest in high-end photography equipment, you have four options:

1. Purchase brand-new camera equipment and gear outright.

2. Purchase used camera equipment from reputable companies, like B&H Photo Video (www.bhphotovideo.com) or Adorama (www.adorama.com), or directly from other professional photographers. As long as a lens is not scratched, its mount is not bent or damaged, and its auto-focus function works properly, you can save a fortune buying used lenses and related gear, including flash units, lens filters, and tripods.

3. Rent equipment for specific shoots or events. Many companies, like Lensrentals. com, CameraLensRentals.com, or BorrowLenses.com, rent camera bodies and

individual lenses by the day, week, or month. Short term, this can help you equip yourself with the right gear for a specific shoot, but this option is not cost effective if you use it often. If you need to rent a specific lens multiple times in a year, for example, you'll save money purchasing that lens new or used as opposed to renting it repeatedly.

4. Borrow a camera body, lenses, or related gear from a fellow photographer. This option is the least expensive, unless you accidentally damage or lose the equipment and need to pay for the repairs or replacement.

It goes without saying that a digital SLR or mirrorless, full-frame camera body is an absolute necessity. However, many professionals believe the camera body is less important than the collection of lenses and related gear you invest in. Regardless of the shooting situation or location, you always want to shoot in the highest resolution possible with the

## ▶ Lights, Camera, Click

When designing a photo studio, part of the process includes deciding what type of base lighting to install. Floor-based lighting is when you have light stands and background supports that are designed to be lightweight and easily portable. Of course, you will need to watch your step so you don't stumble over the lighting equipment or power cords.

A ceiling-based studio has mounted background rollers and a rail system for flexible positioning. It also frees up floor space for your other equipment and furnishings. This is generally the preferred method, although it typically costs more than floor-based studio lighting solutions.

As for how much lighting you will need in terms of watts or brightness (if using LED lighting)— that depends on what format camera is used and how big the subject being photographed is. For example, head and shoulder portraits require much less light than vehicles or other large objects. Keep in mind, LED lighting for studios tends to be less expensive than other pro lighting options, but the end result will depend a lot on the camera and lens you're using with the lighting system.

To keep things simple, many pro lighting manufacturers sell two-, three-, and five-light kits. These kits include the lights, stands, and accessories needed to properly light various types of subjects. B&H Photo Video and Adorama both sell a wide range of individual lights, as well as lighting kits that range in price from a few hundred to several thousand dollars. You'll also find affordable lighting kits available from online retailers like eBay and Amazon.

best quality lenses you can afford. Unfortunately, high-end lenses tend to cost a fortune. It's not uncommon to spend between $500 and $3,000 on one lens.

There are many kinds of lenses, but the three basic types are normal, wide, and telephoto. Event photographers typically use wide aperture lenses, while macro lenses are used for close-up shots of small objects, like flowers or jewelry. Lens filters, like UV or polarizing filters, should be part of your gear and used when needed.

**tip**

Before you purchase an expensive camera body, lens, or related pieces of equipment, borrow or rent it first. Use it yourself on a few shoots to determine if it is worth the investment.

Many photographers are quite comfortable using the lens that came bundled with their digital camera as a general purpose lens but wind up investing in a lens better suited for

## ► Avoid Gray Market Equipment

Anytime you're shopping for cameras, lenses, or related gear online, if you find a deal that seems too good to be true, make sure you're not about to purchase equipment that's refurbished or "gray market" gear, which is equipment sold by anyone other than the manufacturer, often designed for sale outside the U.S. If you decide to go with refurbished equipment, make sure it's been certified as refurbished by its manufacturer and not an independent dealer or reseller. Manufacturer refurbished equipment should come with the same guarantee and warranty as a new item.

Gray market items may be genuine, but they are designed and manufactured to be sold in a different country. In many cases, gray market cameras from companies like Nikon or Canon are vastly different from their U.S. counterparts and are typically not compatible. The power requirements and the materials used to manufacture the gray market camera (or lens) will also be different from what you purchase in the U.S.

While you might save money purchasing a gray market camera or lens, keep in mind that if you needed to get that equipment repaired, the U.S. offices for the manufacturer will not honor the warranty. Thus, getting the item repaired in the future may prove extremely costly and may not even be possible.

Instead of trying to save money by purchasing refurbished or gray market cameras, lenses, or gear, you're better off purchasing used equipment you know has been well cared for and is in perfect working order.

shooting portraits as well as a telephoto lens. Again, the selection of lenses you'll need will depend on the photography specialties you opt to pursue.

Beyond lenses, you'll also need to invest in other must-have gear, such as a flash unit, tripod, and plenty of extra camera batteries and memory cards. You should also never skimp on a good tripod. This is one accessory that you can purchase used and save a fortune. Based on your personal shooting style, however, you may be more comfortable using a monopod. These tend to be more portable and require less space when you're shooting with them. For example, if you're shooting an event, concert, or show, a monopod is much more convenient because it uses much less floor space.

Filters, strobes, and flashes are also important gear you'll want to invest in. Depending on how technical you are when it comes to manually adjusting your camera settings, you may require a light meter as well. Another important investment, especially if you'll do most of your shooting on location as opposed to within your own studio, is a well-designed camera bag that will keep your camera, lenses, and gear organized and well protected.

Keep in mind that it takes a lot more than expensive equipment and a fully stocked studio to be a successful photographer. These are simply your tools; they are not going to turn a mediocre photographer who lacks creativity into a skilled photographer who consistently shoots visually interesting, attention-getting, and professional-quality images.

## Equipping Your Office with the Right Stuff

Once you have your camera, lenses, and gear acquired and ready to use, the next step is to purchase the equipment you'll need to operate your business. When starting a new business, most entrepreneurs love trotting down to the local office supply superstore. It's easy to get carried away when you're surrounded by an abundance of clever gadgets, so discipline yourself to get only what you need. For starters, consider these basic items:

▶ *Computer and printer.* In addition to editing and managing your digital images, your computer will be needed to help you handle bookkeeping, maintain client records, create and manage your website, and perhaps to handle some of your social media-related advertising and marketing.

▶ *Software.* As discussed in Chapter 4, there are many types of applications that can be used to edit, enhance, organize, print, share, and archive digital images. Adobe is a pioneer in creating this type of software that's used by pros around the world. You'll also need general business applications (such as a word processor and

## ▶ Consider Using CRM Software

Instead of simply using a basic contact management application, such as Microsoft Outlook or the contacts app that comes preinstalled on your computer or mobile device, consider investing in customer relationship management (CRM) software.

This type of application allows you to manage all aspects of your interactions with potential and existing customers and clients, plus keep detailed records related to all communications, interactions, and past assignments/work.

Zoho Online (www.zoho.com), HubSpot (www.hubspot.com), Zendesk (www.zendesk.com), and Salesforce (www.salesforce.com) are some of your many options.

spreadsheet). For these, you can use Microsoft Office 365, Google Docs, Apple iWork, or the Open Office applications. Other types of applications you'll likely need to help manage the day-to-day operation of your business include software for bookkeeping/accounting, email management, and contact management/CRM.

▶ *High-speed internet service and cloud storage.* This basically goes along with the computer because it is essential to have access to the internet. Invest in the fastest high-speed internet service that your budget will allow to accommodate the size and volume of images you will be transmitting. Most pro photographers rely on at least one cloud-based service to help manage and archive their digital image library, which will potentially require that you upload and download thousands of images per month.

▶ *Data protection.* You'll also need a data backup system that allows you to copy the information from your computer to another local storage option, such as an external hard drive with 2TB, 4TB, or 6TB of storage capacity. Beyond that, seriously consider using a cloud-based system to backup and archive your images remotely.

**aha!**

Check with companies like Grasshopper (www.grasshopper.com), eVoice (www.evoice.com), FreedomVoice (www.freedomvoice.com), or Phone.com (www.phone.com/features/toll-free-numbers) to obtain an affordable toll-free phone number that can be forwarded directly to your smartphone, home phone, or office phone service.

► *Photo printer.* As a photographer, being able to create professional-quality prints on demand from your home, studio, or office will often be useful, even if you plan to use a professional photo lab to create the prints that you'll sell to customers and clients. A good photo printer will cost at least several hundred dollars, but you also need to consider the cost of replacement ink and high-quality photo paper. A typical photo printer can generate prints up to 8.5 by 11 inches; however, wide-carriage or large-format photo printers are also available. The cost of these can easily go into the thousands.

► *Email.* You'll discover that most of your customers and clients will want to communicate with you via email as opposed to by telephone. It's an essential business tool. As we said earlier, make sure you obtain email addresses that relate directly to you or your business (such as jason@jasonrrichphotography.com or info@jasonrrichphotography.com). Do not use a free email account from Google, Yahoo!, or AOL, for example. Doing this conveys an unprofessional image. Once you have your email accounts established, check your messages regularly and reply to them promptly. You can do this from your internet-connected smartphone, tablet, or computer. As a business operator, consider

## ► Mailing List Managers

There are many software and online-based mailing list managers that allow you to create and manage an email mailing list and then custom-format professional looking emails that are personalized to groups or people on that list or to the entire list. MailChimp (https://mailchimp.com) is just one example of this type of service. iContact (www.icontact.com) and SendGrid (https://sendgrid.com) are two others.

One important function you'll need to provide is the ability for people to sign up for (opt-in) and then later unsubscribe (opt-out) from your email mailing list. Using email management software, this functionality becomes fully automated.

As a small-business operator, email marketing can help you stay in contact with your existing customers and clients, plus reach out to potentially new customers and clients in an extremely cost-effective way. Just make sure that the emails you send are well-written, targeted to your audience, nicely formatted, and free from spelling and grammatical errors. It's also essential that you send emails only to the people who request it. Otherwise, you're sending out spam (unsolicited email), which many consumers will not appreciate.

investing in specialized software that allows you to manage email lists and format emails to look more professional, especially if you plan to embed digital images within your emails.

# Burglar-Proof Your Business

Whether you are homebased or in a commercial location, you need to be sure that your facility is safe and secure for you, your employees, and your clients. Of course, you also want to protect your equipment and any inventory you might have. Most people know that photography equipment fetches a high price, so take protective measures to prevent theft.

## ▶ Batten Down the Hatches

Take preventive steps to protect your computer system from hackers. Imagine that your computer is a brick-and-mortar business stocked with cash, sensitive documents, inventory, and expensive equipment. You're not just going to let somebody walk in and clean you out. You're going to protect your business with an alarm, a padlock, and a safe. Your computer has to be secured in pretty much the same way. Recommended safety measures include:

- ▶ Installing a firewall and virtual private network (VPN) onto your computers. You should also use a VPN with all your mobile devices.

- ▶ Updating your anti-virus and anti-malware software on a regular basis and scanning your computer frequently. Macs are less prone to viruses and malware than Windows-based PCs, but it's still a good idea to have this type of software running on all your computers.

- ▶ Changing your passwords often with a different one for each account. Make sure you never reveal your account passwords to others.

- ▶ Handling online transactions using a credit card (not a debit card). It's also secure to use an electronic payment service, such as PayPal, Apple Pay, Google Checkout, or Samsung Pay, especially when making large online purchases.

Thanks to technology and the growing concern for security issues, the cost of electronic surveillance equipment is dropping. Many insurance companies offer discounted premiums when these devices are installed. You can also increase the effectiveness of your security system by discreetly posting signs in your windows and around your facility announcing the presence of that equipment.

Look into your area's crime history to determine what steps should be taken to safeguard your business. Contact your local police department's community relations department or crime prevention officer to find out if your studio's location has a higher-than-desired crime rate. Most will gladly provide free information on what kinds of security measures are needed. Some will even personally visit your site to discuss specific crime prevention strategies. Many also offer training seminars for small businesses and their employees on workplace safety and crime prevention.

# Help Wanted: Staffing Your Studio

**M**any professional photographers are content running their businesses as solopreneurs, handling everything from answering emails to transporting photography equipment to location shoots and setting everything up. There is nothing wrong with this strategy, but if your plan is to expand your business, there will be a point at which you will need to hire people—second shooters, photography assistants, or office support staff, for example.

Even if your goal isn't growth, there may still be times when you need assistance. Thus, you should know how to find, hire, and manage trustworthy, hardworking, and reliable employees or link up with trustworthy independent contractors.

If you've never supervised or managed people, you may find it difficult to delegate important tasks to someone else. The best way to get around this obstacle is to just do it, knowing that you've done your due diligence when it comes to finding and hiring people you can trust.

It's a good idea to start hiring people *before* you desperately need them. If you wait until the last minute, there is a potential for making hiring mistakes and poor decisions that could cost you dearly, both in terms of cash and quality of service. Keep in mind, a bad employee can ruin your professional reputation with customers or clients.

Another component of the staffing plan is to establish a pay scale. Of course, this depends on what you are hiring people to do, the skills needed, and the salary ranges in your area. You can get a good idea of the pay ranges in your area by talking to other photographers or doing some online research. For example, Salary.com (www.salary.com) is a powerful research tool that can help you determine how much to pay, based on a job description, job title, location, experience, and education level.

To find out national average pay scales for a variety of positions, go to the website for the Department of Labor, Bureau of Labor Statistics at www.bls.gov.

## The Hiring Process

The first step in the hiring process is deciding exactly what you want someone to do. First, create a detailed, well-written job description. You know you need help, but exactly what kind? Do you need someone to monitor the phones and schedule appointments or an assistant to accompany you to location shoots? Perhaps you need an experienced second shooter to assist with wedding or event photography gigs.

A well-written job description should include a job title, then describe, in detail, all job-related responsibilities and expectations, including the physical requirements of the job (such as setting up equipment) and the number of

**aha!**

It's a good idea to have your attorney review the job application you will be using for compliance with the most current employment laws. Your lawyer should also review your job descriptions to avoid any problems related to accidental (or intentional) discrimination.

hours per week the person is expected to work as well as the specific work schedule. Putting this in writing forces you to think about the type of person who will best meet your needs, which reduces the risk of hiring the wrong person. It also gives you something to show applicants, so they can tell if the job you are offering is appropriate for them.

The job description doesn't have to be long and formal, but it needs to clearly outline the person's duties and responsibilities. It should also list any special skills, experience, education, or required credentials (like a valid driver's license and clean driving record for someone who is going to be driving a vehicle as part of their job). They should also be able to pass a background check and drug test, especially if they'll be on location or in a studio setting working with or around kids. See Figure 9–1 on page 96 for a basic Job Description Worksheet.

Before you consider hiring employees, think about how you plan to manage them. Establish basic personnel policies so that potential employees know who's doing what and when they're supposed to be doing it. Don't think that because you're a small company, you can just deal with HR and personnel issues as they come up. Also, don't expect employees to read your mind and understand what they need to do or know what's expected of them unless you're very clear. Do your due diligence and think through your HR plan well in advance of advertising for employees. Pick up Caroline Stokes' *Elephants Before Unicorns: Emotionally Intelligent HR Strategies to Save Your Business* (Entrepreneur Press, 2019).

For example, clearly define what fringe benefits you offer and who is eligible to receive them. Spell out working hours, as well as sick days, holidays and vacation. Explain what conduct is unacceptable on the job and how the disciplinary process works. If you have a dress code, it should be described. You'll avoid a lot of problems if you set policies in advance.

**tip**

Based on your personality type, decide what type of manager you are going to be before hiring someone. If you're a hands-on kind of person, an independent thinker may not appreciate your style. But if you need an employee to take the proverbial bull by the horns, you may be annoyed with someone who requires a lot of feedback.

You should also ask prospective employees to fill out a job application—even if it's someone you already know and even if they have submitted a detailed resume. A resume is not a signed, sworn statement acknowledging that you can fire them if they lie—an application is. The application also helps you verify a resume, so compare the two and make sure the information is consistent.

You can get a basic job application form at most office supply stores, create your own from scratch, or download a template from the internet (via a website such as

# Job Description Worksheet

Date: _____   Job Title: _____

**Objective** (write a brief statement of job's purpose):

_____

_____

_____

Hours per Day/Week/Month: _____

**Responsibilities:**

| Job Duties | Frequency |
|---|---|
| 1. _____ | _____ |
| 2. _____ | _____ |
| 3. _____ | _____ |
| 4. _____ | _____ |
| 5. _____ | _____ |

**Required Skills:**

_____

_____

**Required Education/Knowledge:**

_____

_____

**Required Licenses/Certifications/Permits:**

_____

_____

FIGURE 9–1: **Job Description Worksheet**

## Job Description Worksheet

**Working Conditions:**

- ❏ Seated
- ❏ Stooping
- ❏ Climbing
- ❏ Reaching
- ❏ Other:

- ❏ Lifting
- ❏ Traveling
- ❏ Driving
- ❏ Handling/Setting Up Photo Equipment

_____

_____

_____

_____

FIGURE 9–1: **Job Description Worksheet,** continued

www.formstemplates.com/job-application) and then customize it.

Also, look into working with a background check, credit check, and drug testing company. Make sure each potential employee passes all these checks and tests before making a job offer.

## Building Your Dream Team

One of the biggest challenges for any business is finding and keeping qualified people. Be creative and look for alternatives to the standard ads you can post on ZipRecruiter, LinkedIn, Glassdoor, and Indeed. Those are viable, low-cost ways to attract qualified job applicants quickly with minimal effort, but they aren't the only places to look. You should also network among people you know, check with college

**tip**

Keep in mind, wages are not the only part of an employee's total compensation package. Add more perks to the package by including health insurance, paid holidays, and vacations. An added incentive could be an annual bonus or something as simple as providing lunch when shooting events on location, for example.

**warning**

Correctly classifying workers is important. Failing to do so can result in severe tax-related penalties.

placement offices, and actively participate in industry networking groups.

Flexibility is a key ingredient to finding good people, and there are lots of talented folks who either don't want to work full time or who need to work unusual hours. This type of arrangement can be beneficial when you are just starting and are unsure about your workload. As your business grows and you need to extend the hours or decide a full-time person should do a particular job, you can change the status of that employee. If that doesn't work, consider hiring a second part-timer, setting up a job-sharing situation, or devising some other solution that lets you retain a valuable person and still get the work done.

## Independent Contractors

An alternative to going through the process of hiring full-time employees is to use independent contractors (or freelancers). Of course, there are advantages and disadvantages, but more important, you need to understand the difference so you can avoid unnecessary and costly mistakes at tax time.

As an employer, you will pay payroll taxes, workers' compensation insurance, unemployment benefits, and any other employee benefits you may decide to offer. An independent contractor (or freelancer) is self-employed and will pay their own taxes and insurance and file their own requisite forms with the IRS.

Of course, you have greater control over employees than you do over independent contractors. Employees must comply with company policies and with instructions they receive from you or a manager. You can also set their hours and other conditions of employment along with their compensation package.

If you use independent contractors (or freelancers), you should have a written agreement that describes the services to be performed, the anticipated timeframe in

**aha!**

As soon as you start hiring employees, independent contractors, and/or freelancers, make sure they sign an agreement stating that your company owns the copyrights and retains full ownership to any images shot by those people. It should state that they are shooting on a work-for-hire basis and will retain no legal ownership of their work.

Your employees and contractors should also sign a nondisclosure agreement that prevents them from revealing any details about you, your business, or your clients to others, including your competition.

## ▶ Don't Forget About Workers' Compensation Insurance

In most states, if you have three or more employees, you are required by law to carry workers' compensation insurance. This coverage pays medical expenses and replaces a portion of the employee's wages if they are injured on the job. Even if you have only one or two employees, you may want to consider obtaining this coverage to protect both them and you in the event of an accident.

Details and requirements vary by state. Contact your state's insurance office or your own insurance agent for information so you can be sure you're in compliance.

which they are to carry out those duties, and how much they will be paid. The agreement can also be instrumental in confirming that the person is indeed an independent contractor (freelancer), and not a salaried employee, in the event the IRS or any other government agency questions the working relationship. For more information, consult your accountant or tax advisor. And to find independent contractors, check freelancing websites like Upwork.com, Fiverr.com, Freelancer.com, or Thumbtack.com.

## Short-Term Solutions

From time to time, your staffing needs may fluctuate. This can be especially true around holidays when you may have a backlog of rush orders. Perhaps a special project requires an additional person for a brief interim. Or a regular full-time staff member becomes ill or takes a vacation, leaving a vacancy for a short period.

Before the situation becomes overwhelming, consider using an employment service as a source for temporary help. Many entrepreneurs feel they can't afford the fee, but with the agency handling the advertising, screening, and background checks, the fee is often well worth the investment.

You may also find that certain tasks can be handled by an independent contractor, freelancer, or consultant. If you have tasks you need help with but that don't fit the parameters of a regular part- or full-time position, look for nontraditional ways to get them done.

As a professional photographer who will be operating your own business, keep in mind that you likely won't be able to handle all the necessary responsibilities yourself as your business grows and becomes more successful. Early on, make sure you have the proper infrastructure in place so you'll easily be able to take on more clients and/or larger clients and be able to meet their demands.

## ▶ Consider Hiring College Interns

Many colleges and universities (as well as trade/vocational schools) offer internship programs. Contact your local university or community college to find out what the requirements are for hiring an intern who is interested in learning more about photography or building their portfolio. Most businesses now offer to pay interns but offer compensation that is considerably lower than what a regular employee would receive for doing the same work. However, the intern receives real-world work experience, the ability to expand their portfolio, and college credit. Often, internships are unpaid positions.

Part of the process requires you to complete an application describing the position (this is where the job description comes in handy) and what you need in terms of skill level—beginner, intermediate, or advanced. The school will then try to match you with qualified applicants and send you their resumes for consideration. Typically, the internship program will stipulate how many hours the intern can work each week or month as well as what tasks the student may or may not be allowed to do.

Once the proper infrastructure is in place, one of the fastest and easiest ways to grow your business is to pursue aggressive real-world and online-based marketing and advertising efforts. This is the focus of the next chapter.

# Marketing Made Easy

The success of your photography business relies on much more than just taking captivating and attractive pictures. It also depends heavily on how you market your services. Marketing is the glue that holds your business together and helps it stick in the minds of consumers. To that end, there are four overall marketing-related steps you'll need to accomplish to build a successful business.

▶ First, you need to become a skilled photographer so you can consistently take professional-quality photos related to your specialty.

▶ Second, it's essential to create an eye-catching, attention-grabbing portfolio of your work that you can show to potential customers and clients in the real world, plus proudly showcase online—via your website, social media, and highly targeted online ads.

▶ Third, you need to formally establish your business and kick off targeted and well-thought-out marketing, advertising, and promotional campaigns. What you need to understand is that your marketing, advertising, and promotional efforts must be ongoing. This is what will drive the majority of your business, and when you stop these efforts, you'll discover the influx of new customers and clients will also come to a grinding halt.

▶ Fourth, once you have customers, it's your job to offer top-notch, highly professional, and friendly services so not only will the people you do business with love your photography work, but they'll rave about it to their friends, family, and co-workers, plus return to you when they need additional photography work. For example, if you invest a lot of time and effort booking a gig as the event photographer for a sweet 16 birthday party or bar mitzvah for a family's

## ▶ Discover What Your Competition Is Doing Online

Be sure to visit the websites social media pages, and feeds of other professional photographers. In addition to focusing on the design and layout of their content, pay attention to how their online presence helps to differentiate their work from the competition and showcase their unique style as a photographer.

Since the features and functionality of social media services is evolving quickly, along with what's possible with a website, it's important to stay up to date and make sure you're presenting your content in the most effective and efficient ways possible.

Many of the online services that cater to professional photographers allow you to visit the websites, online galleries, and online presence developed by other photographers. Invest the time to study what other photographers are doing, especially those who are focusing in the same specialty areas. You'll likely discover that the most successful photographers use simple and easy-to-navigate website and online gallery designs.

oldest child, you'll want to do an amazing job. Ideally, you want that same family to hire you again to be the photographer for their two younger children's future sweet 16 parties or bar mitzvahs and perhaps use you for each of their children's senior portraits (and maybe even weddings). Building a positive, potentially long-term relationship with a customer or client could result in plenty of repeat business. At the very least, it can also help ensure you receive positive word-of-mouth advertising from that customer or client, which will also likely lead to new business.

If you learn just one lesson from this chapter, it's that to operate almost any type of professional photography business, both real-world and online marketing is essential. You must be able to clearly define your target audience(s), then devise creative ways to reach them with your cohesive, synergistic, and customized advertising and marketing message and materials. In many cases, the effectiveness of your advertising and marketing will directly impact the long-term success (or failure) of your business based on your ability to differentiate yourself in the marketplace.

## Marketing in the Real World and Online

Marketing, advertising, and promotion for your business needs to be done in the real world as well as online. You'll quickly discover that handling these tasks successfully and in a cost-effective way is a skill set unto itself.

Marketing encompasses a wide range of free and low-cost activities that are designed to promote your business to its target audience. Your website, social media activities, printed sales brochures, and business cards are all examples of powerful marketing tools you should take full advantage of.

One of your main marketing focuses should be on paid advertising to promote your business online as well as in traditional media, such as newspapers and magazines. When it comes to highly targeted, cost-effective advertising, there are many online opportunities that, if used correctly, can generate new customers and clients quickly.

For example, you can do paid advertising using Google Ads (https://ads.google.com), Facebook (www.facebook.com/business/help/1767727736592827), Twitter (https://marketing.twitter.com), and Instagram (https://help.instagram.com/537518769659039). Choose social media services that you know your target audience uses.

If you're a wedding photographer, for instance, part of your ad budget may be used to take part in regional wedding expos and bridal fairs several times each year. It may also make sense to advertise in local or regional bridal and wedding publications.

*Promotions* is another broad term used in business. It can encompass any activities that get the word out about your company to your target audience. The activities that work best tend to be creative, so think outside the proverbial box. For example, you can generate new business as a wedding photographer by developing cross-promotions with local catering companies, florists, bridal gown companies, tuxedo rental places, wedding cake bakeries, disc jockeys, and wedding band managers. These are all companies that are targeting the same audience as you but are not direct competition. Why not come up with ways to work together and help generate business for each other?

If you're a portrait or fine art photographer, consider contacting a few local coffee shops, restaurants, and businesses that serve customers (including doctor's offices). Offer to provide them with free, professionally framed prints that they can hang on their walls in exchange for being able to post a small sign next to each image that displays your name, website, and contact information.

The business that displays your photography receives free artwork to decorate its walls, and you receive free promotion. Some local businesses will sell your prints for you, right off their walls, which offers yet another source of revenue for you as well as serving as a promotional tool.

Online, a promotion might involve offering discounts for photography packages on your website, such as 20 percent off holiday portraits if booked before October 1, or providing a free engagement photo portrait sitting when a client books you to shoot their wedding.

Some marketing, advertising, and promotional activities can be fun because you can tap your creativity. However, most of these activities will require you to develop a budget, crunch numbers, track progress, and tweak campaigns on an ongoing basis. For example, if you're doing paid online advertising, you'll be provided with real-time analytics that show who is seeing your ad and how they're responding to it based on keywords, search phrases, and other targeting criteria.

The goal with any type of advertising, especially online advertising, is to spend the least amount of money but generate the best possible results in the shortest amount of time. To achieve this, it's necessary to learn how to read and understand the analytics data you're given as well as how the online advertising vehicle works, then fine-tune your campaign(s) as needed to achieve better results.

Regardless of your budget, the most important thing to keep in mind is that marketing, advertising, and promotions are an important and ongoing investment in your business. We'll explore these further later in this chapter. But first, think about an organic way of spreading the word about your business—networking.

## aha!

To help you learn more ways to use word-of-mouth advertising to your advantage, check out the resources offered by The Association of National Advertisers (www.ana.net).

# Network, Network, Network!

Word-of-mouth from friends, family, business acquaintances, and your past customers/clients will be one of your best and most reliable sources for promoting your photography business. Tell everyone about your new venture and ask for their help in spreading the word about it.

In addition to real-world connections, many people you know probably have dozens, hundreds, or even thousands of online friends via social media. In other words, they're "influencers." A simple but positive mention on someone's Facebook page or Twitter feed could help you generate new business.

The more you can get people talking about you and your business, the better this form of viral or buzz marketing can work. Best of all, word-of-mouth advertising is free. It just requires that you consistently offer top-notch customer service and invest the time to build positive business relationships with the people who can help spread the word about your business. For business-to-business marketing, especially if your specialty is corporate photography, services like LinkedIn can be very useful marketing tools.

## *Join Professional Associations*

Join local associations, organizations, and civic clubs, especially those affiliated with photography or any other business communities that you can share information, resources, and services with. The American Society of Media Photographers (www.asmp.org), for example, offers educational programs and networking opportunities through more than 39 chapters across the U.S.

Find out when your local chamber of commerce, Rotary Club, or Toastmasters group holds meetings that

## tip

The internet is changing the way people shop for photographers, just as it is changing everything else, according to trade groups such as the Professional Photographers of America. If you'll be operating a studio, you'll want to add a listing for it on services like Yelp!, Google Maps, and Apple Maps. You can also seek new customers or clients by advertising locally on online services like Groupon (www.groupon.com/merchant/join). And if you'll be specializing in weddings, you may want to join your fellow photographers by advertising and maintaining a listing on The Knot (www.theknot.com).

you can attend, and exchange business cards with new acquaintances. There is a wealth of information you can learn from small-business owners in other industries who have successfully carved out a niche for themselves.

## Get on Your Soap Box

Make yourself available as a speaker to every professional, fraternal, and service organization in town. Many of these groups meet weekly, and they are always looking for speakers. You may not get paid, but you'll often get a free meal, make some valuable contacts, and get the word out about your business. You can also become an instructor for regional adult education programs, offering lectures, workshops, or classes that teach an introduction to digital photography or photo editing, for example.

When giving talks, keep the information you provide helpful but general—don't make this a sales pitch for your business. Have business cards and brochures on hand to distribute at the end of your presentation.

Get a list of all the organizations that might be receptive to having you speak, and send a letter introducing yourself. Some examples are:

- ▶ 4-H clubs
- ▶ Church groups and events
- ▶ Garden clubs
- ▶ Kiwanis Club
- ▶ Nature clubs
- ▶ Parenting groups (such as your local PTA or PTSA)

The chamber of commerce or public library can provide you with a more comprehensive list of networking opportunities within the community.

If you want to do a more in-depth presentation, consider offering seminars. Seminars help your market learn more about what services you offer and give you an opportunity to showcase your work while sharing valuable information.

For example, if you're a wedding photographer, you could offer a free seminar about how to hire a wedding photographer or how to create the perfect wedding album.

Being in front of an audience gives you the opportunity to show, not tell, what you are all about. If someone is interested enough to attend a free seminar on how to hire a wedding photographer, if you impress them with your presentation, chances are they'll choose your service when it comes time to hiring the photographer for their wedding. The goodwill that comes from giving your market something for nothing is immeasurable, and it can go a long way toward building client loyalty.

Consider offering free seminars at your local library or through your city's adult education (or continuing education) program. If you specialize in Bar Mitzvah photography, offer a photography seminar at local Jewish Community Centers, or if you offer wedding photography services, offer a seminar at local bridal or wedding shows, for example.

# Advertising and Public Relations

Advertising and public relations are two key ways you'll promote your business to the public locally, regionally, nationally, or even globally. Where and how you choose to advertise will depend on your budget, photography specialty, target audience, and goals. Let's dig into some of the techniques common in the photography industry.

## *Direct Mail*

Because of its ability to target well-defined geographical areas, direct mail is an effective way to promote your photography services. In fact, direct mail (using the U.S. Postal Service instead of email) is experiencing a comeback, lest you think it is a thing of the past. According to the Direct Marketing Association, the direct-mail response rate in 2018 was 5 to 9 percent greater than its digital marketing counterparts, with a 9-percent response rate for mailers sent to house lists (mailings sent to residences). That's a decent ROI. However, depending on your target audience, you may find it much more cost effective to use online advertising or email marketing instead. For example, younger people (in their 20s or 30s) will typically respond better to email and online marketing, while older people (over the age of 50) often respond better to direct mail, since this demographic tends to be less active online.

There is no magic formula when using direct mail, except using a solo mailer is more successful than including your information in a cooperative mailer full of supermarket coupons. Depending on what services you offer, you can send a flashy postcard, informative brochure, or sales letter with a personal touch. In most cases, the costs associated with acquiring a mailing list, printing, and postage fees will be higher than using a targeted online ad or email campaign that will likely

**aha!**

An online service, called Postable.com, allows you to communicate with your potential or existing customers/ clients by sending them personalized, seemingly handwritten note cards, letters, or postcards. This is one way you can promote sales, offer a "thank you" for recent business, or attract new customers with a well-written sales letter.

generate business faster. It all depends on the audience you're trying to reach and the marketing message you're trying to convey.

Postcards generally get more attention than letters. However, with a sales letter, you can include a response card that encourages prospective clients to contact you for more information.

Mailing lists can be purchased from list brokers, which you can find online. These lists come in just about every category, and since you've hopefully done your marketing homework when creating your business plan, you already know the lists you want based on the target audience(s) you're attempting to reach.

As a Bar Mitzvah photographer, you want to reach Jewish families (with kids under the age of 13). If you're a wedding photographer, you need to reach engaged couples who are planning a wedding. As a pet photographer, your target audience is pet owners (typically dog or cat owners). Event photographers need to reach people hosting or planning events, such as birthday parties, graduation parties, engagement parties, holiday parties, high school or college reunion parties, or retirement parties, where the host wants to hire a professional photographer to document the event.

Add value to your direct mailer by presenting some sort of bonus offer. Put something in the ad that will draw in new customers, perhaps a 20-percent discount or $20 coupon for the purchase of a studio package. This can be an excellent way to generate business.

## Replace Yellow Pages with Online Maps

Printed phone books or printed Yellow Pages directories are not used as widely as they used to be, so unless your target audience is an older crowd, advertising in a local or regional Yellow Pages is no longer a good use of your advertising or marketing budget. In fact, if you ask a 20-year-old what the Yellow Pages are, chances are they'd have no clue.

### ▶ Make Contact with Coupons

If you're not feeling altogether flush, a viable direct-mail alternative is a coupon mailer that groups retail businesses within a community. The coupon books or packages are mailed nonselectively to all homes within a specific zip code, so they aren't as targeted as a direct-mail piece that you'd design yourself, but they can still have great pull.

As a business owner, you pay a fee to the company producing and distributing the coupon books or packages. Valpak (www.valpak.com/advertise/products-services/direct-mail-coupons) is just one example of this type of marketing tool.

Instead, make sure your business and website is listed with popular search engines and your photo studio, if applicable, maintains an accurate listing on Yelp!, Google Maps, Apple Maps, and other similar services. This is important if you need to attract local customers to actually visit a business or studio location.

If you still think Yellow Pages advertising makes sense for your target audience, placing your listing under the right category is critical so people can find you. You will also increase the chances of a potential client seeing your business name if you insert your listing under multiple headings or categories.

## Business Cards

As small as they are, business cards are a powerful marketing tool. Hand out these little gems at every opportunity. Think of them as mini-billboards that tell people who you are, what you do, and how to reach you.

Whenever you meet someone—in church, at your kids' school, in the grocery store, waiting in a lobby, at a business meeting, or anywhere else—and the subject of what you do for a living comes up, hand over your business card as you describe your company. As a matter of fact, give people two cards—one to keep and one to pass along to someone else.

A quick-print shop can do a nice, affordable job on your business cards by providing a variety of templates to choose from. You can also order them online from companies, like Vistaprint (www.vistaprint.com) or Canva (www.canva.com), for a nominal charge.

Your business card should look professional. Choose multicolor printing on a good quality business card paper stock. The cards should also showcase your logo and prominently display your website address, social media links, phone number, and physical address (if you operate a studio).

## Press Releases

Press releases can generate free publicity opportunities that expose your business to the community, but to be printed in the media (such as a newspaper), the information has to be newsworthy. One way this subtle form of self-promotion can be done is by tying the announcement into local or national events, community programs, or holidays. A local or regional newspaper might also consider featuring a profile or an interview with you as a new business operator.

A press release must be created in a standard format. You can hire a freelance public relations specialist to help create attention-getting press releases, or you can download templates online. Your press release should quickly answer the following six questions: who, what, where, when, why, and how, plus have a local or regional twist. Keep in mind, a press release is not an advertising tool, so the wording you use should be less sales-oriented and more promotional and informative.

**tip**

Be sure to ask every client and prospective client how they heard about you so that you can track the effectiveness of your marketing efforts.

Within your press release, provide interesting information that gets straight to the point by letting readers (reporters, journalists, editors, or producers) know how this announcement will benefit their audience. Although you are essentially advertising your business, you want to avoid this type of slant because self-promotion is not considered newsworthy.

Make up a list of media contacts, including television, radio, newspaper, and community organizations so when you are ready, you can send out a press release blitz. Be sure to include your contact information. Folks in the media work on tight deadlines, and if they can't reach you right away to ask questions, they may be inclined to drop the story and move on.

In addition to targeting mainstream media outlets, send your press releases to bloggers and vloggers who target the same audience as you. These people are considered "social media influencers" and often have large and loyal followings. You might consider offering a blogger, vlogger, or social media influencer a free photo shoot in exchange for their help promoting your business to their audience.

## Television/Radio

Television and radio can be effective in your marketing strategy if you're advertising something concrete, like a holiday promotion or a special event. It also helps if you're advertising locally, where you know potential customers are listening to your chosen station.

## ▶ Charitable Donations

Depending on your photography specialty, offer to donate portrait sitting packages, a complete wedding photo package, or a selection of framed prints as a charitable donation for auctions or fundraisers. Choose one or more charities that you're personally passionate about so you share a common interest with everyone who attends the charity event.

In exchange for your donation, the charity will often promote your company in a variety of ways in addition to offering your donation(s) as prizes.

Again, understand who your target audience is. Many people spend their free time streaming content from the internet and using services like Hulu, Sling, Netflix, YouTube, and the like. It's possible to advertise on YouTube, and you may find this to be a powerful way to reach potential customers. To learn more about YouTube advertising opportunities, visit www.youtube.com/ads.

Meanwhile, just as the TV watching habits of consumers have changed dramatically in recent years, so have their radio listing habits. When people listen to the radio, it's not always local radio stations, thanks to the SiriusXM Satellite radio service that's now available is most vehicles as well as from stand-alone radios, smart speakers, and mobile devices. Paying to advertise on a local AM or FM radio station no longer has the reach it once did, so as a small-business operator, you'll likely discover more effective ways to spend your ad budget.

**tip**

Don't just focus on print publications. More and more consumers are opting to read niche magazines online as well as online-only publications. These, too, allow you to reach a specialized audience in a cost-effective way.

## *Magazine and Publication Ads*

Magazine and publication ads seem to be only minimally effective for photographers. In addition, they are sometimes expensive and can be hard to get responses from unless they are carefully crafted with an explicit call to action. That's usually achieved by promoting a specific product, service, or information. If you opt to use this form of advertising, add an incentive, such as a discount if a client contacts you and mentions seeing the advertisement, or include a coupon as part of your display ad.

### ▶ Consider Paid Podcast Advertising

If you want to reach a niche audience, consider advertising on a podcast. Pinpoint a handful of podcasts that cater to your market and reach a lot of people. You can find podcasts about almost any topic imaginable using a podcast directory, then easily determine the size of their respective audiences. Popular podcast directories include iTunes (Apple Podcasts), Stitcher, TuneIn, Spreaker, Luminary, and Google Play Music. How much you'll pay to advertise will depend heavily on the size of the audience and the podcaster's popularity.

Use niche publications that match your business. For instance, a commercial photographer can use architectural or interior design magazines. Advertising in local newspapers is another way to create public awareness of your business, although readership may be limited. Chances are your city or state has its own parenting publication, so if you're advertising family portrait, birthday, party, event, or bar mitzvah photo packages, these publications might help you target the perfect audience.

## Designing and Publishing Your Website

Once you acquire your business's domain name (as you read about in Chapter 7), such as www.jasonrichphotography.com, you then need to design and publish a website and populate it with impressive content. As a business operator, first consider the goals for your website. Will it be used simply as a marketing tool to showcase a sampling of your work, or do you want it to also handle a variety of other tasks?

For example, potential customers can use your website to:

► Review your work (your portfolio) and learn about the types of services your company offers.
► View your company's pricing.
► Schedule an in-person or phone consultation, or a portrait sitting, for example.
► Buy images and/or photo products online with their credit or debit card.
► Preview images taken at their event, party, or wedding, for example, and choose their favorites or request specific edits to be made.

The appearance of your website is important. It must look extremely professional. If you invite potential clients to an amateur-looking website that's poorly designed, complicated to navigate, and contains spelling and grammar mistakes, people will assume that your photography work is equally amateurish and not hire you.

The good news is that you do not need to become a programmer or professional website designer to create and maintain a professional-looking and fully functional website. Plenty of website hosting services and turnkey website services for professional photographers provide all the tools you need to design

**tip**

Be sure your website address and social media links are printed on your business cards, within all your promotional materials, as well as displayed within your ads. Not only can your website serve as a powerful sales tool, but it should also be used as a portfolio to showcase your best work.

your website with easy-to-use templates. Once you choose a template that offers the appearance, layout, and functionality you desire, you'll simply add your own logo, text, and images—and your website will be up and running within days.

If you're not tech-savvy, consider hiring a freelance website designer/graphic artist. You'll still need to provide a logo, text, and portfolio images, but you won't have to handle anything technical to get your website published and operational.

The majority of turnkey services charge a flat monthly fee and provide the online-based tools needed to design, publish, and manage a website. Extra fees will apply if you want to transform your website into an ecommerce site to directly sell products and/or services online.

**tip**

In addition to focusing on your website's design so it appeals to your target audience, make sure you use a reliable website host provider to ensure your website stays online 24/7 without technical or service glitches.

Some website services for photographers are already affiliated with online-based photo labs so you or your customers can place orders for prints, enlargements, or photo products. Some allow you to publish multiple portfolios and/or create and share separate, password-protected online albums/galleries with specific clients.

One of the first things you should do is visit at least a dozen different websites for professional photography businesses. Determine what design elements and functionality you like and want to offer on your own site, then choose a turnkey service that offers those features and functions for a reasonable fee.

Following are just a few of the website turnkey services for photographers that offer the tools needed to create, publish, and manage a full-featured, professional-looking website:

- ▶ Jimdo(www.jimdo.com)
- ▶ PhotoDeck (www.photodeck.com)
- ▶ SmugMug (wwww.smugmug.com)
- ▶ Squarespace (www.squarespace.com/tour/photography-websites)
- ▶ Weebly (www.weebly.com/photography-websites)
- ▶ Wix.com (www.wix.com/html5us/photographer)
- ▶ Zenfolio (https://zenfolio.com)

When evaluating the various services, focus on the features and functions offered, the pricing, the reputation, and the appearance of sample websites hosted by the service.

Once you start designing and planning your website, be sure it clearly showcases your company logo, you as the photographer, and your best work. It should also clearly describe

## ▶ Test Drive Your Website Frequently

As you're designing your website, consider that many of your visitors will be accessing it from computer monitors of varying sizes as well as the much smaller screen sizes of their smartphones and tablets.

Your website should be easy to read and auto-format each page based on the screen size it's being viewed on. After all, more and more people are using their smartphones and tablets to surf the web and visit websites to learn about businesses and services. There are still plenty of people, however, who might visit your website using their computer or perhaps access it from a Smart TV that's connected to the internet. As a result, you want your content to look perfect, regardless of what screen size it's being viewed on.

On a regular basis, you should test your website by accessing it from different size computer screens and mobile devices to make sure everything looks perfect.

In addition, while all web browsers are supposed to be compatible and display web pages the same way, this is not the case. Install all the popular web browsers on your various computers and mobile devices, then test your website using each of them. The most popular web browsers include Microsoft Edge (for Windows PCs), Apple Safari (for all Macs and iOS mobile devices) as well as Google Chrome, Mozilla Firefox, and Opera.

Since the programming used to operate web browsers changes often, you want to periodically check how your website looks using popular web browsers on your computer (Microsoft Edge, Safari, Chrome, Firefox, etc.), plus make sure it continues to look good when viewed from mobile devices after a major operating system or web browser upgrade.

To help you quickly test your website using multiple web browsers across all popular hardware platforms, you can subscribe to and use a fee-based service, such as SmartBear CrossBrowserTesting (https://crossbrowsertesting.com).

what services you offer and provide simple answers to the most common questions potential customers will have about your business. Your website should also promote your social media accounts, and your social media feeds should promote and link directly to your website.

Make sure that every page of your website displays your phone number and email address so potential customers and clients can easily contact you when they're ready. Keep in mind the majority of your potential customers and clients will visit your website *before* calling or hiring you. Others may call you first but then review your online portfolio before deciding to hire you. Thus, your website should serve as the perfect sales and marketing tool for your business. Put in the time, money, and effort to create a website you're proud of and will exceed the expectations of those who visit it.

## Don't Underestimate the Power of Online Social Networking

Becoming active on social media (Facebook, Twitter, Instagram, Pinterest, Snapchat, LinkedIn, YouTube, etc.) is a low- or no-cost marketing strategy that can have a global impact while building personal relationships and credibility.

As a small-business operator, it's not a question of whether you should become active on social media, it's a question of which social media services you should become active on. This is a decision you should make based on your target audience and their online habits.

The popularity of social media services ebbs and flows. Facebook continues to have more than 2 billion active users worldwide but has come under scrutiny related to how it's using user data, so some people have opted to stop using Facebook in favor of other services. Meanwhile, young people were once hooked on using Snapchat but have since migrated to Instagram. Depending on your target audience, identify which social media services they use most frequently, then set up free accounts and become active on those services.

Ideally, you want to create separate accounts on each service for your business. You don't necessarily want to mix your personal social media activities with what you're doing professionally. In other words, create a separate Facebook page for your photography business, which you can then promote using your personal Facebook page, for example.

**aha!**

When making any design decisions or choosing specific features and functions to incorporate into your website, put yourself in your target customer's shoes. All design and content decisions should be made based on what your target audience will appreciate and respond well to. This includes everything from the layout and functionality to the color scheme and the fonts you use to display text. When choosing a website template that you'll customize, choose one that will appeal to your audience and showcase your photography skills and work in the best possible way.

Participating on social media is free, but it involves a time commitment. Use it to build an audience for your work and to showcase it to the masses as well as to attract potential customers or clients. If you discover that your target audience actively uses social media services like Facebook, Instagram, and Twitter, you may discover that doing paid advertising (also referred to as paid promotions) on these services, in addition to the content you publish for free, is a worthwhile investment.

**aha!**

For information on how to create a Facebook Business page, visit www.facebook.com/business/pages.

Social media advertising is typically a low-cost online advertising option that can be highly targeted and will allow you to reach your audience very quickly. You're also able to see free, real-time analytics that show you how well your online ads are performing.

Alexi Killmer frequently promotes her Child Essence Photography business on Facebook by featuring weekly specials and images. "I've also used Craigslist (www.craigslist.org) quite a bit to offer packages at discounted prices," she says.

Another advantage of social networking is that you can build profiles to enhance your visibility and link back to your website. While it's true that social networking can be time consuming, it can also be effective when done consistently. Set aside a specific time each day to create and publish content on social media and to respond to other people's posts. Become active in online discussions related to the type of photography work you do, and use these forums to answer questions and engage potential customers. The biggest investment will be your time, so you don't want to waste it.

## Portfolios

Your website should feature an online portfolio that showcases your best work and relates directly to your photography specialty. However, you also want to maintain a traditional (printed) portfolio so you can showcase your work during in-person meetings with perspective customers or clients.

Many photographers use a laptop computer or tablet to digitally present their portfolios during sales meetings with prospective customers or clients. There are apps that allow you to easily create digital slideshows of your portfolio as well as interactive portfolio software applications or cloud-based services that can be run on a laptop computer or tablet based on your needs.

If you have the need to present a professional looking portfolio of your work online, or during an in-person presentation or sales pitch, for example, there are many portfolio services that allow you to showcase your image in an eye-catching, interactive, and highly professional way.

A few of the many online-based photography portfolio services include:

▶ PhotoShelter (www.photoshelter.com)
▶ SmugMug (www.smugmug.com)
▶ Squarespace (www.squarespace.com)
▶ Viewbook (www.viewbook.com)
▶ Weebly (www.weebly.com)
▶ Wix (www.wix.com)
▶ Zenfolio (www.zenfolio.com)

Keep in mind that the features and functions offered by each service, the technical know-how required to use them, the selection of website/gallery design templates, and the pricing to use each service varies greatly.

**aha!**

In addition to the framed photographs that are hung for display, also offer unframed images for sale. This gives you the opportunity to sell a less expensive item to budget-conscious consumers as well as to exhibit other images that might not be included in the booth's theme. To appeal to a higher-end crowd, consider selling metal, acrylic, and/or canvas prints as well.

## Art Shows and Galleries

A number of photographers make their living solely by exhibiting in major art shows and festivals, while others may do it seasonally. It's not an easy process. Participating in art

---

### ▶ Use Email Signatures as a Marketing Tool

Email signature lines are important and should be at the bottom of every email message you send out. They should comprise approximately four to five lines with your name, company name, website address, social media links, and a short list of your services. Your photo and logo can also be displayed.

Several online-based services will help you format and create professional-looking email signatures that will automatically get pasted to the bottom of every email message you compose or respond to.

Check out services like Sigstr (www.sigstr.com) or Black Pearl (www.blackpearlmail.com/supercharge-your-email). For specific tips on how to design an attention-getting email signature, visit www.getmailbird.com/10-examples-professional-email-signatures-businesses.

shows and festivals often requires a lot of travel and the loss of your weekends, but it can be a rewarding experience.

It's generally recommended that new art exhibitors start at local events sponsored by community groups, schools, and churches. Once you have some experience and are feeling comfortable exhibiting your work, move on to state and regional shows for more exposure.

Keep in mind, the bigger shows have higher entry fees and more stringent requirements. For these shows, there are typically more applications than booths, and there is no guarantee you will be accepted. The best quality shows and festivals are juried by a panel of experts who determine who can participate from their applications and submitted slides, so make sure your submissions are your best work.

## The Initial Process

Before applying to some of the better art shows, attend them first to see what other photographers are exhibiting and how they are displaying their work. Not just anyone can jury into an art show. The competition is fierce on two levels: first, for space to show your photographs; and second, for sales.

The application process usually starts months in advance and requires hopeful exhibitors to submit a biography or resume, the application, an application fee, a jury fee, and a sample portfolio.

You can find out about art shows and festivals from other exhibitors, as well as through your local chamber of commerce. For information on regional and national shows, look at the Art Fair SourceBook (www.artfairsource.com). Another useful publication is the *Sunshine Artist* magazine (www.sunshineartist.com), which is an in-depth magazine for major art shows and festivals.

## On the Circuit

Once you've been accepted to a show or festival, find out what will be provided and what you will need to bring. If the festival takes place outdoors, exhibitors usually provide their own canopies, which can be purchased or

**aha!**

One way to grab the attention of people who visit your booth is to set up a large-size HD monitor that's linked with your computer or tablet so you can present an animated slideshow to showcase your best work in a continuous loop.

Check out this website to learn about the highest-rated digital signage software that can help you create your presentation: www.capterra.com/digital-signage-software.

rented. Whether you are exhibiting indoors or out, you will also need to provide display racks or fabric walls on which to hang your photographs. Other important considerations are incidentals, like a comfortable chair, display tables, and bins.

If you'll be selling your work, you'll need to set up a credit card merchant account so you can quickly process credit and debit card payments (as well as electronic payments via PayPal, Apple Pay, or Google Pay). Companies like Square (https://squareup.com), PayPal (www.paypal.com/us/webapps/mpp/payment-methods), and Intuit (https://quickbooks. intuit.com/payments) all offer easy and low-cost ways to set up a credit card merchant account that involve no long-term contracts.

## The Appearance of Your Booth Is Important

Next, think about how you want to present your photographs to their best advantage. If there is a row of 150 booths, what do you have that will draw in browsers to look at your images?

You also have to think about what photographs work well together as a unified body. It's not enough to simply throw a bunch of your favorite pictures together and hang them up. If buyers are looking at a wall featuring a wedding, a landscape, and a building design, they are going to be confused. Decide who you are marketing to and give those images the wall space they deserve. Keep in mind that your booth basically functions as a mini showroom, and an attractive set up helps customers visualize how a certain piece will look in their home or office.

## Galleries

Another option for pro photographers is to showcase your work within galleries. "It's pretty difficult getting into the better-known galleries initially," says Jerry Clement. "One way to build your reputation is to approach new gallery owners who may be looking to represent unknown but talented artists."

The application process is very similar to applying for an art show: You submit the required paperwork

**tip**

Use nonglare glass on framed prints. It's more expensive than regular glass, but it doesn't reflect everything, making it easier for prospective buyers to see the image. Showcasing images printed on metal is also a good way to go, because it looks professional and slick. Companies like Nations Photo Lab (www.nationsphotolab. com), Shutterfly (www. shutterfly.com), and Bay Photo Lab (www.bayphoto. com/wall-displays/ metalprints) are just a small sampling of online-based photo labs that can create metal prints at affordable prices.

## ▶ Trade Shows and Conferences

Trade shows and conferences can be a tremendous opportunity for learning—or a huge waste of time. There are two types of shows: consumer, which focus on home, garden, and other consumer themes, and business-to-business, where exhibitors market their products and services to other companies. You can likely benefit by attending, and perhaps even exhibiting, in both.

For example, if you are a wedding photographer, consider exhibiting in a wedding show expo or a women's trade show, like the Southern Women's Shows (www.southernshows.com). Commercial photographers can set up booths at building and remodeling expos, such as the International Builders Show (www.buildersshow.com).

You can find trade shows scheduled throughout the country at Tradeshow News Network (www.tsnn.com). Whether or not participating in trade shows is worthwhile will depend on your target audience, the services you offer, your budget, and your goals.

(sometimes with a fee) by the registration deadline along with copies of your work for approval (sometimes by a jury). Gallery images are typically displayed for up to a month, unless you are applying for permanent representation.

Unlike an art show, you are not required to be present at the gallery during operating hours, which takes a lot of pressure off the artist. If one of your images sells, gallery personnel handle everything from collecting the money to delivery of the product, while tucking away a commission for their part in closing the deal.

## Kill 'Em with Kindness

You are your best marketing tool! Nothing can beat good old-fashioned customer service. The internet has changed the face of photography and business in countless ways, but it still hasn't changed the need for a

**aha!**

There are many ways you can market your photography skills without being obtrusive. One amateur photographer put a couple of 5 x 7 prints in nondescript picture frames and hung them on her cubicle wall at work. Because they were of good quality and attention-getting, visitors noticed them right away and asked questions about where they originated. She ended up selling several prints for $30 each and was commissioned by a co-worker to take pictures at her son's bar mitzvah.

small-business operator to offer superior and friendly customer service—in person, on the phone, via email, and through each and every interaction.

According to Kenneth Salzmann, a photojournalist and writer who began his career in the 1970s, "The internet can and does open many new doors, but what keeps them open is an old-fashioned commitment to customer satisfaction—the level of quality, responsiveness, integrity, and timeliness that makes today's client a repeat customer."

Holding on to a client for the long run is not only good for business but also a good business practice in and of itself. Adds Salzmann, "It costs more than meets the eye to lose a customer."

# Crunching the Numbers: Finances and Taxes

The best indicator of how serious you are about your photography business is how you handle your money. Basically, there are two sides to the issue of money: how much you need to start and operate and how much you can expect to take in. Doing this type of research is often difficult for photographers who would rather be out in the field or in the studio doing their work as opposed to being bound to a desk crunching numbers, working with spreadsheets, or tinkering with bookkeeping/accounting software. But to be successful, part of your responsibility is to successfully manage your money. In this chapter, we'll cover the basics you need to know to stay in the black and keep doing what you do best.

## Startup Funds

As noted earlier, many photographers start out part time and eventually segue into a full-time business as time and money permit. This gives entrepreneurs the opportunity to generate sufficient income to cover expenses and make a profit without borrowing funds, at least initially.

**tip**

Before starting a new business venture, you should first have some capital in the bank. The rule of thumb is to have enough money to operate the business and support yourself (and your family) for at least three months. You should also have enough capital set aside to buy whatever equipment you are going to need.

How much money you need in the beginning depends on a number of factors, such as whether you will be homebased or in a commercial studio and how much photography equipment and gear you need to initially purchase. Other costs to consider and calculate into your budget include inventory, supplies, licenses, permits, marketing, and operating capital needs (the amount of cash you need on hand to carry you until your business begins generating income). Use the Startup Costs Worksheet in Figure 11–1 on page 125 to help estimate how much money you're going to need.

After figuring out how much money you're going to need to launch your business and get it running successfully, you'll have to consider where the money will initially come from. Some of the options include:

▶ *Personal resources.* When thinking of creative ways to come up with startup funds, do a thorough inventory of your financial assets. Make a list of what you have, including savings and retirement accounts, equity in real estate, vehicles, collections, life insurance, and other investments. Though you may not want to sell your car or siphon funds from your retirement account to finance your photography business, you may be willing to sell that vintage Seiki Canon camera for a few thousand dollars. It's just collecting dust anyway. But if you don't want to sell your assets for cash, think about using them as collateral for a loan.

▶ *Credit cards.* Many successful businesses have been jump-started with plastic. Just be smart about it because sky-high interest rates could bury you for years. If you

## Startup Costs Worksheet

| Expenses | |
|---|---|
| Mortgage/Rent | $ |
| Utility Deposits | $ |
| Upgrade/Remodeling | $ |
| Photography Equipment and Gear | $ |
| Computers and Tech Equipment | $ |
| Wide Format Photo Printer(s) | $ |
| Office Equipment | $ |
| Office Supplies/Materials | $ |
| Licenses/Permits | $ |
| Accounting/Legal fees | $ |
| Advertising/Marketing | $ |
| Vehicle | $ |
| Owner/Operator salary | $ |
| Payroll | $ |
| Insurance (first quarter) | $ |
| Miscellaneous | $ |
| | |
| **TOTAL** | $ |

FIGURE 11–1: **Startup Costs Worksheet**

use a credit card to help fund your photography business, only charge items that will contribute to revenue generation. Many business books frown on using credit cards to finance a new business venture, mainly because if things go bust, you'll likely be on the hook personally to pay off the debt (with high interest) to the credit card companies. A few late or missed payments, and your personal credit rating will be destroyed for at least seven to ten years.

**tip**

You want to make a good impression when applying for a loan, and that includes presenting your company's materials in a businesslike manner. Assemble and organize all your paperwork in a professional folder or portfolio along with any relevant brochures and price lists. Banks and investors will be looking for a comprehensive, well-written, and well-thought-out business plan.

▶ *Friends and family.* A lot of startup businesses have been funded with seed money from friends and relatives who recognized the potential value of the venture and who wanted to help their loved ones succeed. However, be cautious with these arrangements. No matter how close you are with the potential investors, present yourself professionally, put everything in writing, and be sure the individuals you approach can afford to take the risk of investing in your business. Never accept money for a business venture from anyone who can't afford to lose that money. Also, consider what will happen to your relationship with those people if your company doesn't succeed and the investors wind up losing some or all of the money they invested.

▶ *Partners.* Using the "strength in numbers" principle, look for someone who may want to team up with you in your venture. You may choose someone who has financial resources and wants to work side-by-side with you in the business. Or you may find someone who has money to invest but no interest in doing the actual work. As with your friends and family, be sure to create a written partnership agreement that clearly defines your respective responsibilities and obligations.

▶ *Government programs.* Take advantage of the abundance of local, state, and federal programs designed to support small businesses. Make your first stop the SBA (www.sba.gov/funding-programs), then investigate various other government and private programs. Women, minorities, and veterans should check out niche financing possibilities designed to help them get into business. The business section of your local library or the internet are good places to begin your research.

▶ *Lending institutions.* While banks might seem like the most likely sources of financing, they are generally the most conservative. Besides wanting to know exactly what the money will be used for (shown in your business plan), they usually require some type of collateral, such as real estate, a life insurance policy, stocks, bonds, or a savings account. If you have excellent credit, you may be able to take out a signature loan for a few thousand dollars, although the interest rate will be higher than on a traditional loan.

**warning**

Most business financing experts agree that you should never obtain a second mortgage on your home to finance your startup business. If you do this and the business doesn't succeed fast enough, you run the risk of having your home foreclosed on and losing it.

If these more traditional routes do not provide the funds you need, you can also consider options like crowdfunding or seeking venture capital. Be mindful, however, that both come with risks. Crowdfunding (an offshoot of asking friends and family for money) can have unpredictable results. You may get several hundred people to contribute, or you may only get a handful of donors. As for venture funding, you may need to pitch an idea that is broader than a simple photography business. If, however, you have a unique contribution to the industry (say, a concept for a specialty photography business that has franchise potential), then a venture pitch might be the right move for you. You can read all about your funding options in *Finance Your Business* (Entrepreneur Press, 2017).

**tip**

The SBA recommends that businesses in general—photographers among them—budget adequately for marketing, advertising, and promotion to make sure they are reaching potential customers. When starting a business, plan on spending *at least* 10 percent of your expected annual revenue on these efforts.

## Financial Management

Once you are up and running, it's important to monitor your financial progress closely, and the only way you can do that is by keeping detailed records. You can handle the process manually; however, there are a number of excellent bookkeeping and accounting applications you can use. For example, there's Intuit's QuickBooks (www.quickbooks.com) and Oracle's NetSuite (www.netsuite.com), which are the leading accounting and booking applications used by small businesses in a wide range of industries. A few other options include FreshBooks (www.freshbooks.com), Wave (www.waveapps.com), and Zoho Books (www.zoho.com/us/books).

Whatever accounting system you use will help you produce financial statements that tell you exactly where you stand and what you need to do next. The key financial statements you need to understand and use regularly are:

**tip**

If you carry a balance on a credit card that is used solely for business purposes, the interest is deductible, but if you mix business and personal charges on the card, the interest is not even partially deductible. Consult with your accountant to learn more about possible credit card interest deductions before filing your taxes.

- ► *Profit and loss statement* (also called the P&L or the income statement). This statement illustrates how much your business is making or losing over a designated period—monthly, quarterly, or annually—by subtracting expenses from your revenue to arrive at a net result, which is either a profit or a loss. Initially, this document may not be of much value to you, especially during the startup phase. But over time as your profit history grows, you will appreciate this useful management tool.

- ► *Balance sheet.* A balance sheet is a table showing your assets, liabilities, and capital at a specific point. A balance sheet is typically generated monthly, quarterly, or annually when the books are closed.

- ► *Cash-flow statement.* This summarizes the operating, investing, and financing activities of your business as they relate to the inflow and outflow of cash. Its main purpose is to point out when the cash flow isn't flowing so you can work out a solution and pinpoint trouble spots in the future. As with the profit and loss statement, a cash flow statement is prepared to reflect a specific accounting period, such as monthly, quarterly, or annually.

Successful business owners review these reports regularly, at least monthly, so they always know where they stand and can quickly move to correct minor difficulties before they become major financial problems. If you wait until June to figure out whether you made a profit last December, you will not be in business for very long.

Once you have a fiscal system in place, your next step is to open a separate checking account for your business so that you don't commingle personal and business funds. You will also need a business credit card or at least a separate credit card in your name that you use exclusively for your photography business.

# Tax Matters

Businesses are required to pay a wide range of taxes. Make sure you keep detailed and accurate records so you can offset your local, state, and federal income taxes with the expenses of operating your company. Making a tax-related mistake can be costly when you consider the penalties and interest charges you can incur by your state and the IRS.

For example, if you have employees, you'll be responsible for payroll taxes. If you operate as a corporation, you'll have to pay payroll taxes for yourself; as a sole proprietor, you'll pay self-employment tax. Then there are property taxes, taxes on your equipment and inventory, fees and taxes to maintain your corporate status, your business license fee (which is really a tax), and other lesser-known taxes. Depending on what you're selling, you may also be required to collect and pay sales tax.

You must report all income from your photography business, no matter how insignificant. Failing to do so is a crime. If a government bean counter starts poring over your books, a defense of, "I didn't think you would catch me," or, "Oops, I didn't know I needed to pay taxes on revenue generated by my small, startup business," isn't going to be much value if you are caught not reporting income.

Of course, in addition to reporting all your income, you should take every deduction to which you are legally entitled. Homebased businesses may qualify for the home office deduction, which allows you to deduct a portion of your rent, mortgage interest, household utilities and services, real estate taxes, homeowner's insurance, repairs, security systems, and depreciation. If you're driving back and forth to the post office, regularly go on other business-related errands, or you drive yourself to on-location photo shoots, you can either deduct mileage or depreciate your car and write off the actual expenses.

Also, be sure you charge, collect, and remit appropriate sales tax on your products and services. To

**warning**

Congress passed the Tax Cuts and Jobs Act (TCJA) in 2017, which went into effect in January 2018. The TCJA impacts a wide range of deductions and exemptions for businesses both large and small. Be sure you are up to date on the changes that will affect your bottom line. For the latest updates, visit www.irs.gov/tax-reform.

**tip**

Use your invoices as a marketing tool. Add a brochure or promotional flier to the envelope. Even though the invoice is going to an existing client, you never know where your brochures will end up, and you should always strive to earn repeat business from existing customers.

do this, you'll need a sales tax ID number, which you can usually get by simply filling out a form. Check with your state's department of revenue for information on how to get a tax ID number. Make sure that you review all your tax liabilities with your accountant.

## How Will You Get Paid?

An important part of financial management is setting up an easy-to-manage account receivables system. This includes establishing clear and appropriate policies that are fair to your clients and protect you.

As part of their billing practices, many photographers extend credit by systematically generating invoices or monthly statements. This task can be easily handled with bookkeeping software, like QuickBooks, that include a basic invoicing module.

If you choose to custom-design your own invoices and statements, be sure they're clear and easy to understand. Detail each item and indicate the amount due in bold, with the words "Amount Due" in front of the total. A confusing invoice may be set aside for clarification, and your payment could be delayed.

Decide when payments are due and make that a clear part of your policy statement. Your policy should also address how far an account may be in arrears before you suspend services to that client or turn over the debt to a collection agency. This is always a tough call, but remember that you are a for-profit business, and if you don't get paid, you can't pay your own bills, earn a salary, and generate a profit.

### Accepting Credit and Debit Cards

Whether for convenience, security, reward points, or out of habit, many of today's consumers prefer to pay with plastic. Most small-business owners find it helps if they are able to accept credit and debit cards. Fortunately, it's much easier to get merchant status than it has been in the past; in fact, these days merchant status providers are competing aggressively for your business.

To get a credit card merchant account, you no longer need to start with your own bank. Shop around! It's worth taking the time to get the best deal.

**aha!**

On your contract, include a statement describing the methods of payment (cash, credit cards, checks, or electronic payment services) you accept. This will depend on the credit card merchant account provider you work with. Many turnkey website services offer an ecommerce solution that will include handling credit card, debit card, and electronic payment service transactions.

Services like Square (https://squareup.com), PayPal (www.paypal.com), Venmo (www.venmo.com), and Intuit (https://quickbooks.intuit.com/payments) provide easy-to-set-up merchant account services that have no long-term contracts. They charge competitive fees only when you use the service to collect payments. These merchant account services are typically compatible with the ecommerce components of most turnkey website services, but make sure this is the case before choosing a provider.

Many of the social media services also now allow you to sell products and/or services directly from your online-based account and accept credit card payments via the service (or using Apple Pay, PayPal, or another electronic payment service). If your advertising and marketing focus is on establishing a social media presence, determine if you'd benefit from being able to accept online payments for products/services directly through these services.

When dealing with tech-savvy consumers, you'll likely discover that offering these electronic payments via apps and services, such as PayPal, Apple Pay, and Venmo, will provide an added convenience to your customers and clients, plus help to ensure you get paid faster.

## Accepting Checks

Although paying by plastic is dominating the payment market, many of your clients may prefer to write you a personal check. (This also applies to businesses that may pay you the old-fashioned way.) Businesses lose billions of dollars annually because of bad checks, so look for several key items when accepting them.

Check the date for accuracy. Do not accept a check that is undated, postdated, or more than 30 days old. Be sure the written amount and numerical amount agree. Post your check acceptance procedures in a highly visible place at your studio and in your contract, invoice, and/or agreement. This listing should also include the steps you will take (and the fees you will charge) if a check is

**aha!**

Corporate clients you bill on a regular basis may appreciate the convenience of having their credit cards automatically charged each month so they don't have to write a check—and you don't have to wait to get paid. If you're a wedding or event photographer, though your clients will often pay you in installments and many will prefer paying for your services using a credit card or debit card (or an electronic payment service such as PayPal, Apple Pay, or Venmo).

You will, however, have to pay a small percentage of the sale to the credit card merchant account service provider.

returned for nonpayment. Most clients understand the risks you take when accepting checks and will be willing to follow your rules.

If most of your clientele are local to your community and you're providing services in a middle- or high-income area, the risk associated with accepting checks is much lower. You always have the option, however, of initiating a "no personal checks accepted" policy.

## What's in the Forecast?

You don't need a crystal ball to predict future revenue, but you need a formula to foresee how much you can expect to make in the weeks, months, and years ahead as these numbers will become your sales goals. Pay close attention to and use your key financial statements on a routine basis. Plan for the costs of growth, and watch for signs of developing problems so you can figure out how to best deal with them before they turn into a major crisis. Developing analytical foresight demonstrates that you are an astute business owner on top of every situation.

# The Price Is Right: Knowing the Value of Your Art

**B**eing a professional photographer is half creative visual artist and half astute businessperson. Clients are under the impression when they purchase your photographs that they are buying an image or product. But they are acquiring your experience, expertise, creative vision, and understanding of the assignment neatly packaged in a 5-by-7-inch print or digital proof. In essence, your services are your product.

A lot of variables come into play when establishing fees and rates for your photography business. Two of the most significant considerations are your specialty and geographical location. An event photographer's fees are predictably higher in Seattle, Washington, than Madison, Wisconsin due to the cost-of-living factor. On the other hand, the event photographer in Madison will most likely have a more thriving business than a fashion photographer in the same area because of better opportunities. However, if the fashion photographer were willing to travel to metropolitan areas, like Seattle, the event photographer would probably be left crying in the dust.

Determining a feasible pricing structure is one of the most daunting tasks a new photography entrepreneur faces. There's not a magic formula when deciding how much to charge for your work, but there are some helpful guidelines you can follow.

## Pricing Strategies

In a world of easy digital imaging for the masses, photographers are finding new challenges when it comes to getting a fair price for their work. That may mean that they will have to get creative and change the rules of pricing to better serve their bottom line.

The proliferation of digital media has made it much harder to charge for prints in the traditional way. So rather than adopt a "nickel and dime" pricing strategy where you charge for each print of an image (or for a photo shoot, proofs, photo album, and/or prints), consider charging only for what clients really value—your ability to capture moments. One way you can capitalize on that is by offering specials on your social media accounts. For example, many family photographers offer "mini sessions" themed to various holidays or times of year via their social media channels. Sign-up is made available to social followers only, and the price is a set one—usually a basic sitting fee for a small package of photos.

A photographer's estimate is usually based on two elements: creative fees and expenses. On the creative side, you need to think about the quality of the image and what value you place on it. Jerry Clement explains that his formula for gallery prints includes the cost of production

**tip**

Use the price point appeal psychology to capture potential customers. For whatever reason, a $49.99 portrait sitting fee sounds so much better than $50. Likewise, discounts rounded to even numbers, like 10 or 20 percent, seem to work better than odd figures, like 15 percent.

and what he calls an "intrinsic, artistic value," with some profit margin on top of that. He says, "You also have to take into account the gallery's commission, which usually averages 30 to 40 percent."

Like most portrait photographers, Alexi Killmer charges a sitting fee when working with clients. "The sitting fee covers my time as the photographer, editing of images, and a private online gallery of the client's photos they can share with family and friends, so they, too, can place orders for prints and photo products," says Killmer.

As part of your fees, factor in labor, supplies, and materials. Will the images be shot on location or in a studio? If you are operating a studio, take a long, hard look at your local competitors to see what they are charging for similar services, then start your pricing somewhere in the middle.

**tip**

Cradoc fotoSoftware (www.cradocfotosoftware. com) is one of several software applications to help freelance photographers with their pricing strategies. Using a database of statistical pricing information, you can estimate appropriate fees for a specific project by keying in several job-specific factors.

Wedding, portrait, and event photographers have an easier time scoping out the competition because it's easy to stop by and pick up a price list and other information from competitors or simply visit their respective websites. Although it's simple enough to pick up the phone and call a commercial photographer about their fees, it's highly unlikely you will get a standard rate because fees are usually developed on a project-by-project basis.

Commercial photographer Ray Strawbridge explained that new clients usually want to know what everything is going to cost before you ever do anything. "And until you do the work, you don't really know," he explains. "But if you have to speculate on a project, and you're not a complete idiot, you're going to pad it because you never know what you're going to run into."

This will be a wobbly balancing act in the beginning, until you have a handle on pricing formulas. You don't want to be the highest priced photographer in town, but neither do you want to run bargain-basement specials that destroy any chance of earning a profit. People have a habit of equating quality with cost, but they also like getting a good deal. In essence, you want there to be a high perceived value without pricing yourself out of the market.

Location shoots are more complex and involve considerations like site logistics, travel, special equipment, lighting equipment, props, and additional personnel (e.g., models, assistants, technicians). In addition to the complexity of the project, the photographer also needs to consider the number of finished images needed, scheduling, and pre- and post-production time.

Pre-production responsibilities may include client meetings, site location and/or visits, and set arrangements. After the shoot is over, post-production tasks may consist of restoring a site to its original state, returning props and equipment, and more client meetings—along with image editing, selecting, and finalizing the images.

Many commercial or location photographers charge day or half-day rates, with fees adjusted to weekly for long-term shoots or hourly for shorter projects. Don't forget to add overtime (hourly rate plus 50 percent) for days that go longer than eight hours or for weekend assignments.

Whenever in doubt, use the industry standards found through different photography associations and organizations, like American Society for Media Photographers (ASMP) or Professional Photographers of America (PPA). Local chapters have monthly meetings where members can network and learn a wealth of information, including local marketing and industry standards.

"A lot of photographers have trouble understanding the value of their work in the beginning," says Michael Weschler. "But it's important to protect your intellectual property. If someone wants to pay you $500 for an image, but they want all rights, you can end up selling yourself short. If it's a really good image that you could potentially resell each time the embargo period ends, you might make $5,000 on it instead."

A usage fee model is often used when working with stock agencies. Ideally, you will be affiliated with a reputable agency that will sometimes tell you who the client is. Even if they don't, they will still give you the parameters of how the image will be used.

Ray Strawbridge sums it up like this: "If it's a stock image you own and can license to somebody simply for usage, like an editorial publication, then that is pretty cut and dried. If they put it on the front cover, it's one fee; if they put a quarter page inside the magazine, it's another fee," he says. "The fee is based on the circulation of the magazine, the size, and the position it will be used. The more times they are going to use it, the more insertions and the larger circulation of the publication, then the more that image is worth."

One of the misconceptions that many people have is that commercial photographers, for example, sell pictures. The reality is, you don't. You license the use of your images. That means keeping track of your images and how clients are using them, while maintaining the copyright and ownership of them.

# Expenses

The other part of the pricing equation is expenses. Many photographers—especially in the beginning—try to absorb minor expenses, like supplies, postage, and basic camera gear. But these little things quickly add up and chip away at your profits. Your fee structure should cover these incidentals. For example, if you decide $50 is a fair hourly rate, charge $75. Then use the hourly charge to calculate daily and weekly rates.

Overhead should also be a calculated expense that includes rent, utilities, insurance, gas, mileage, and anything else that you are not billing clients separately for. Big ticket expenses for individual assignments, like travel, equipment, or personnel, should be billed separately, depending on your—or the client's—preferences.

Photographers often go into the profession out of a love for the art or science of it, but sometimes they overlook a basic business imperative, according to a host of industry experts who have made "cost of doing business" (CODB) a key part of the advice they offer.

Remember, if you forget to include your own salary in your cost of doing business, then you've made a grave business error. Don't just decide to pay yourself whatever is left over at the end of each month. Instead, pay yourself first. Consider the rest of your costs as overhead. Ultimately, if your business can't cover its payroll and expenses, you'll need to charge more for your work, find other ways to increase revenue, and/or cut costs.

After factoring your costs into your pricing structure, find ways to reduce those costs and increase profits. Monitor your progress each month by using profit and loss reports, which your bookkeeping or accounting software should allow you to generate with ease if you're using it correctly. You can use the Profit and Loss Quarterly Report template shown in Figure 12–1 on page 138 to help you keep track.

# Bids, Estimates, and Deposits

It's important to understand the difference between placing a bid on a project and giving an estimate. A bid indicates that you are willing to do the assignment for a set price, whereas an estimate indicates how much you think a project will cost and allows for wiggle room. Whether you're providing a client or customer with a bid or an estimate, it should always be put in writing, signed, dated, and have an expiration date. In other words, the price is only valid for a pre-determined time period.

Once your client accepts your bid or estimate, you should get a firm commitment from them. One way to do that is to collect an advance deposit before starting a

# Profit and Loss Quarterly Report

| INCOME | Jan | Feb | Mar | Qtr |
|---|---|---|---|---|
| Services | $ | $ | $ | $ |
| Product sales | $ | $ | $ | $ |
| Gross profit | $ | $ | $ | $ |
| **EXPENSES** | **Jan** | **Feb** | **Mar** | **Qtr** |
| Rent/Mortgage | $ | $ | $ | $ |
| Utilities | $ | $ | $ | $ |
| Phone (Cell/Office/Fax) | $ | $ | $ | $ |
| Equipment | $ | $ | $ | $ |
| Computer | $ | $ | $ | $ |
| Insurance | $ | $ | $ | $ |
| Vehicle | $ | $ | $ | $ |
| Travel | $ | $ | $ | $ |
| Taxes/Licenses | $ | $ | $ | $ |
| Payroll/Benefits | $ | $ | $ | $ |
| Advertising | $ | $ | $ | $ |
| Repairs/Maintenance | $ | $ | $ | $ |
| Legal/Accounting | $ | $ | $ | $ |
| Photography Supplies | $ | $ | $ | $ |
| Office Supplies | $ | $ | $ | $ |
| Professional Development | $ | $ | $ | $ |
| Postage/Shipping | $ | $ | $ | $ |
| Printing/Copying | $ | $ | $ | $ |
| Internet Service | $ | $ | $ | $ |
| Web Hosting | $ | $ | $ | $ |
| Miscellaneous | $ | $ | $ | $ |
| Total Expenses | $ | $ | $ | $ |
| Gross Net Profit (Loss) | $ | $ | $ | $ |
| Taxes | $ | $ | $ | $ |
| Net Profit (Loss) After Taxes | $ | $ | $ | $ |

FIGURE 12–1: **Profit and Loss Quarterly Report**

project. Traditionally, 50 percent is collected before commencement of the assignment with the balance due on completion. Of course, there are exceptions depending on your specialty. A wedding photographer usually collects a nonrefundable retainer of 25 percent with the balance due *before* the wedding date. The photographer may also set up a payment schedule so the balance can be paid down in increments.

## Crunching Numbers Is an Important Part of the Job

If you want to become successful and grow your business, this will require you to handle tasks you don't like, including bookkeeping and accounting. Many photographers think of themselves as "creative types" who don't deal with numbers. However, if you don't understand the finances related to your business and maintain proper records using accounting or bookkeeping software, you'll quickly find yourself in financial crisis.

**warning**

The photographer must be committed to work on schedule; otherwise, the client will have the right to terminate the contract and look for a more reliable photographer. Naturally, there may be unavoidable delays due to illness, power outages, or other unforeseen circumstances; there should be language addressing those conditions in the contract.

Also, knowing what you're worth in the current marketplace is essential. By differentiating yourself in your field and developing your own brand and photography style, you'll find it easier to charge premium rates for your work. Do your research to determine what your competition is charging as well as what's unique about what they're offering. Next, do whatever you can to offer something better (not necessarily cheaper) to your customers or clients.

# Photographer Beware: Legal Issues in the Industry

B efore stepping out into the world of business, it's important to understand some of the legal concerns that photographers might be faced with and what remedies are available. Otherwise, you might be left vulnerable to personal or professional liability, loss of income, and damage to your reputation.

In this chapter, we'll cover some of legal issues most critical to your success as a professional photographer.

# Copyright Issues

A photographer owns the copyright to their images from the moment of creation, according to the Copyright Act of 1976. Once you click the shutter, you are the creator and copyright owner without having to register it. This means if unauthorized use of an image occurs (and it frequently does), the photographer could be entitled to compensation.

However, if it's not registered and someone uses it without permission, the only thing you can collect are usage fees. If the image was grossly infringed on and you feel entitled to additional compensation, including attorney's fees, you will not be able to collect punitive damages without a copyright registration.

People who blatantly infringe on copyrights know this. They know the cost of pursuing a settlement could be cost prohibitive, so there continues to be a tremendous benefit to registering your images for copyright protection.

Be sure to visit the Library of Congress, Copyright Office (www.copyright.gov/registration/photographs/index.html) for instructions and guidelines on how to file for legal copyrights for your images. As you'll discover, this process can be handled online. For general information about copyrights, visit: www.copyright.gov/help/faq/index.html.

## *Handle with Care*

The reality is copyright infringements are going to happen, but in most cases, it comes from the infringer simply not knowing the rules attached to usage rights. If you find someone who is using an image without authorization, it's important to handle the situation professionally. Try to negotiate a financial settlement before pursuing potentially costly legal action.

## *Protective Measures*

Although using a copyright notice on your photographs is no longer necessary to safeguard your work from copyright infringement, doing so may still be a good idea, according to the National Press Photographers Association.

**stat fact**

Copyrights have a long shelf life. Any work that was copyrighted on or after January 1, 1978, is protected from the date of creation until 50 years after the creator dies. Once a copyright expires, the work (or image) becomes public domain and anyone can freely use it.

Under current law, your work is copyrighted as soon as it is created, but using a copyright notice (i.e., ©2019 Jason R. Rich. All rights reserved.) may be important because it informs the public that the work is protected by copyright, identifies the copyright owner, and shows the year of first publication.

For many professional photographers who specialize in commercial, fashion, advertising, product, or event photography, dealing with copyright infringement continues to be a huge issue, especially when it comes to the internet and having copyrighted images show up on the web. Even if you don't mind if other website owners use your images, they at least need to tell readers/viewers who the photographer is (provide a photo credit) and potentially provide a link to your website.

These days, many photographers put a watermark on the image to establish ownership. This can easily be accomplished using many professional photo editing applications such as Photoshop. There are also applications, such as Photopolish ($39.99, https://photopolish.co), that are designed specifically for adding a watermark to digital images, allowing you to choose the watermark artwork as well as the size and location where the watermark appears within each image.

**aha!**

Michael Weschler recommends signing up for the free service Google Alerts (www.google.com/alerts) so you are notified whenever an image associated with you (and you receive photo credit) is posted online or your name is mentioned. He explains, "It's great because I know when new things are published, which makes me happy to see that I'm getting some new press or exposure."

Most photographers also upload images to the internet using a much lower resolution than they were shot in. This ensures that the picture will have a poor, grainy quality if someone tries to blow it up or print it, for example. It's always a good idea to add metadata to your digital image files that identifies you as the photographer and image copyright owner.

As an added measure of protection, you can include a script within your website's programming so that if someone attempts to right-click and copy one of your images, a friendly reminder pops up to let people know they need to ask for permission first.

## When Do You Need Permission?

Technically, you can shoot anybody or anything you want on public property so long as it's used for an editorial purpose and you are informing people about something that is a matter of public interest. Of course, there are exceptions to this rule, such as private events.

You should always be aware of potential problems when shooting other people or on private property. Some public areas, such as parks or beaches, also restrict professional photographers from shooting unless they acquire a permit. This usually requires paying a small fee and filling out appropriate paperwork. Do your research before just showing up for a location shoot.

No matter what kinds of limitations and disclaimers you attach to that image, you may not always have control over how it will be used in the hands of someone else. It's better to be safe than sorry and obtain the proper releases. Look at the Sample Model Release Form in Figure 13–1 on page 145.

# Get It in Writing

It is good business practice to get any agreements or permissions in writing, and it doesn't have to be incomprehensible legal mumbo jumbo. Photography assignments, freelance agreements, or work-for-hire jobs are no exception. While the word "contract" may sound intimidating, it does not have to be a complicated process. However, it does need to clearly address any and all issues relevant to the proposed assignment or project. Terms and conditions may vary from one project to the next, but the following topics should always be considered:

▶ *Assignment.* Provide a detailed description of what the assignment/project consists of. Are these editorial images to be used in publications, a commercial assignment to promote a client's products or services, or an event, such as a wedding or bar mitzvah?

▶ *Duration.* The contract should state the exact date(s) this assignment should take place. Is this a one-day event, is the assignment expected to cover several days, or is this an ongoing project?

▶ *Location.* Has the location been predetermined, or will the photographer need to research and scout for appropriate sites, venues, or surroundings? If the latter, the photographer will need to bill the client for the additional time involved.

▶ *Additional equipment, props, or models.* Many shoots require the use of professional models or special props and equipment. If the photographer is responsible for obtaining these, then the client should be billed separately.

▶ *Copyright/Ownership.* Unless this is a work-for-hire assignment, photographers generally retain the rights to their images while granting limited usage to the client.

▶ *Fees.* Fees will differ from one assignment to the next. In the contract, be sure to stipulate when payment is expected (e.g., upon receipt of invoice or 30 days after

## Sample Model Release Form

Name of Photographer: _____

Address: _____

_____

Phone: _____

Today's Date: _____

Description of Assignment: _____

Location: _____

For valuable consideration received, I hereby permit the above photographer to use, reproduce, sell, and resell any pictures taken on this day of me, to be used for advertising, art, trade, publishing, or any other lawful purpose within any online, electronic, or print-based media.

I further waive the right to inspect or approve these images or the text that may be used in connection with them. All digital image files or negatives, together with the prints, shall constitute the photographer's sole property.

I am 18 years or older:  Yes _____     No* _____

Model's Name (print): _____

Address: _____

_____

Phone: _____

Signature of Model: _____

Date: ___/___/___

*Form must be signed by parent or legal guardian if model is under the age of 18.

Signature of Parent/Guardian: _____

Date: ___/___/___

FIGURE 13–1: **Sample Model Release Form**

receipt) and if there will be a late-fee penalty. Attach a fee schedule for the client's use.

▶ *Deposits.* Depending on the scope of the project, advance deposits may be required in the amount of 25 to 50 percent. Specify in the contract what portions are non-refundable and when the final balance is due. For example, a wedding photographer usually requires the balance to be paid in full before the ceremony, whereas a commercial photographer will not invoice the client until after the project has been completed.

▶ *Travel and expenses.* The client is responsible for any expenses incurred by the photographer during the commission of this assignment, including hotel, rental car, airfare, mileage, equipment, etc. If the photographer anticipates the expenses to be significant, they can require the client to pay them in advance or obtain a deposit to be applied toward the estimated expenses. You may also want to negotiate a per diem, which would cover incidental expenses such as meals.

▶ *Creative judgment.* Typically, an authorized representative of the client will be present at a shoot to answer questions and instruct the photographer regarding the desired images. In the event a designated individual is not available, add a clause to the contract stipulating that the client must accept the photographer's judgment in the creation of the images.

▶ *Completion date.* State when the client can expect to have the desired images in hand.

▶ *Rescheduling/changes to an assignment.* Sometimes an assignment needs to be rescheduled or changed for a variety of reasons. Specify what additional fees will be incurred in these instances, including any expenses related to the change.

▶ *Cancellations.* Clearly spell out in the contract what the client is responsible for in the event of a cancellation. Will all or a portion of the deposit be withheld? How many days can a client give notice of cancellation before additional fees are

**tip**

The American Society of Media Photographers (www.asmp.org) has sample contracts, agreements, and other useful forms for its members on its website. If you sign up for the free newsletter from SLR Lounge, you can get contract templates from their website (www.slrlounge.com/ photography-contract-template). For a fee, you can also download, print, and use a variety of photography-related business contracts available from HoneyBook (www.honeybook.com/ photography-contract-template).

imposed? Usually the closer to the scheduled date, the higher the penalty. Don't forget to include charges for any expenses that have been incurred.

▶ *Liability.* There should be a clause in the contract that holds the photographer harmless against any claims, liability, or damages that could arise from the client's misuse of the images.

▶ *Previews.* If the client is given proofs or previews to review, make sure they understand these images are the property of the photographer unless stated otherwise.

As always, it's a good idea to bring in a legal expert when you are crafting basic agreements and permissions documents to use in your business. Typically, you can create basic boilerplate language for every kind of agreement you plan to use and tweak it as necessary depending on the client and situation.

# More Expert Advice from Experienced Pros

Nothing teaches as well as the voice of experience. In this chapter, you'll read all about other photographers in the industry who have forged the path you're about to embark on. To begin, let's talk basic advice. The following are six core lessons that pro photographers need to learn early on:

149

1. *Be prepared!* Consider the requirements of each shoot and make sure you have all the equipment, gear, and accessories you'll need (including plenty of charged batteries and blank memory cards for your camera). Also, for extremely important, time-sensitive shoots, like weddings, bar mitzvahs, and corporate events, always have a second, backup camera and lenses with you in case something goes wrong with your primary equipment.

2. *Use props when necessary.* Use live props in a photo shoot to create the ultimate realism, capture the attention of a child, and be able to charge a premium for this type of booking. However, unless the "prop," for example, is a beloved family pet, there are also some disadvantages that should be taken into consideration. Unfamiliar animals (including cute bunnies and baby chicks) bite, scratch, and poop. Some animals require special care beyond that of a traditional house pet or could be unintentionally harmed by an over-enthusiastic child who is squeezing too hard.

**aha!**

An alternative to a live animal is using a fake animal as a prop—many of which look realistic and require minimal fuss. Plus, they can be easily cleaned and last for years. This would also work if you're trying to create a dramatic scene with a less-than-desirable prop, such as a reptile or rodent, or some other creepy-crawly thing.

3. *Don't quit your day job until you know your business will be successful.* There are going to be peaks and valleys in the photography business—especially when you're starting out. This can be a very profitable business venture, but it can be difficult for any small-business owner. To become successful, you'll need to be disciplined and dedicated. When you're not working on an assignment, you should be focusing on other aspects of running your business, such as advertising, marketing, and promotions.

4. *You can create quality prints without a photo printer.* Investing in an expensive, high-quality photo printer can be cost-prohibitive; however, there are alternatives. There are plenty of professional-quality, online-based photo labs that can create prints, enlargements, and photo products for you and your clients. Do some research, place a few sample orders with various labs, then choose two or three you want to work with based on quality, pricing, turnaround time, and services provided.

5. *Get smart.* There are a lot of things photographers don't know about but could learn by attending seminars, classes, and workshops related to photography, and small-business operations as well as marketing, advertising, and promotions. Pursue

## ▶ Business Relationships with Online Labs

One of the ways you can boost your revenue when working with consumer clients (as opposed to companies) is to offer a wide range of prints, enlargements, and photo products. A photo product is any item, such as a metal print, acrylic print, canvas print, photo book, greeting card, mouse pad, smartphone case, coffee mug, or T-shirt, for example, that features your images.

Many online-based photo labs will create high-quality, professional-looking photo products that you design online and can feature your digital images. The products can then be shipped to you or in some cases drop-shipped directly to your customers.

Do some research to determine what types of photo products you want to offer to your customers and clients, then choose at least two or three different online-based labs or services to work with based on their pricing, quality, turnaround time, and product selection. You'll discover that some online-based labs work with both consumers and professional photographers, while others cater to the needs of pro photographers and studio operators. For example, ShootProof (www.shootproof.com) is a full-service company that offers website and online portfolio design and hosting services. Integration with a professional-quality photo lab is built into their offerings.

Some online-based labs or photo product services have specialties. For example, Blurb (www.blurb.com) offers software-based tools and remote printing services for creating professionally printed and bound photo books that you can design using templates or from scratch. Hardcover, softcover, and "imagewrap" cover options, along with a variety of book trim sizes and paper qualities are available.

Metal prints, acrylic prints, and canvas prints not only look amazing but offer terrific profit-generating opportunities for photographers who shoot portraits and events (like weddings or bar mitzvahs). Services like Nations Photo Lab (www.nationsphotolab.com), SmugMug (www.smugmug.com), Full Color (www.fullcolor.com), AdoramaPix (www.adoramapix.com/metal-prints-sem), Bay Photo Lab (www.bayphoto.com/wall-displays/metalprints), and Mpix (www.mpix.com/products/modern-metal-prints) all offer a wide range of services suitable for pros.

Using a quick internet search, you can also find online-based photo editing services. If your photo editing skills—using tools like Photoshop—aren't yet up to professional levels, consider subcontracting your photo editing tasks. Another option is to hire part-time college interns who are pursuing a degree in photography and who specialize in photo editing to assist you with this time-consuming task. Photo editing requires training, skill, creativity, and a lot of practice.

ongoing training and education. For example, MasterClass (www.masterclass.com) is a high-end, online learning service that has teamed up with several award-winning and world-renowned photographers to offer a variety of in-depth, higher-level photography training programs that go well beyond what you'd typically find on YouTube.

6. *Honesty is always the best policy.* In other words, don't try to sell yourself as something you're not. Always be truthful with potential clients about your expertise and experience. If you've been asked to take on an assignment you're unfamiliar with, let them know this is new territory. Offer a steep discount for the opportunity to try. People will appreciate your integrity. Honesty speaks as loud as any photograph!

# More Wisdom from Experienced Professional Photographers

Now, let's hear directly from the experts. The rest of this chapter contains several in-depth and exclusive interviews with experienced professional photographers who pursue different specialties. From these interviews, try to learn from each person's experiences and follow their advice when it's applicable to avoid common mistakes and increase your chances for success.

## *Meet Molly McCauley, Owner/Lead Photographer at Molly + Co.*

Molly McCauley (www.mollyandco.com) is the owner and lead photographer of Molly + Co., a Los Angeles, California-based wedding and lifestyle photography business. McCauley has been voted one of the top five wedding photographers in Los Angeles by CBS. McCauley is also the cofounder of Brand Camp (www.brandcampretreat.com), an organization for female entrepreneurs looking to grow their businesses.

When asked what made her pursue a career as a professional photographer, she replied, "When I moved to California in 2007, I was the first assistant to a wedding coordinator and was introduced to the wedding industry that way. In 2009, while I was obtaining my master's degree, a number of my friends were getting married. I photographed one wedding, and then another, and another, and finally thought to myself—I might have something here. I always say that wedding photography chose me, not the other way around. I love weddings, and I love photography, so the chance to combine these passions and make that my life's work was very appealing."

McCauley has a bachelor's degree in individualized studies with a focus on design, retail merchandising, and photography from the College of Liberal Arts at the University of Minnesota, Twin Cities. She later obtained her master's in fine art photography from Brooks Institute.

From this interview, you'll learn more about the wedding and lifestyle photography business and discover what it takes to be successful in these highly competitive fields.

*What camera equipment do you use?*

*McCauley*: "I use Canon digital gear, including the Canon 5d Mark IV, III, and II, in association with a variety of fixed lenses. My favorite lens is a 50mm. I was trained in film exclusively for years and have experience in medium and large format, including 4x5. I most commonly shoot with a Contax 645 for personal, workshop, or editorial work. If I'm traveling with little space for gear, I choose my Leica D-Lux."

*In the next two to three years, do you believe it will be necessary for all professional photographers to upgrade to full-frame, mirrorless digital cameras?*

*McCauley*: "For professional use, I feel full-frame is always the way to go, as you have the most opportunity and information available to you in digital form. While I have yet to switch my professional gear to mirrorless, I can definitely see the appeal to a lightweight and more compact camera body that packs as much punch as a larger DSLR."

*Beyond being able to take pictures, what additional skills are needed to become a good wedding photographer?*

*McCauley*: "First and foremost, you have to love people and their stories. That's what gets me excited as an artist . . . to capture love with my camera. It takes a special personality to be able to handle all aspects of wedding photography. If you have what it takes, I say go for it!"

*What is the biggest drawback and best perk of being a wedding photographer?*

*McCauley*: "The biggest perk is that you get to share the most precious memories of people's lives with them in a way they could not create themselves. The biggest drawback is dealing with the dynamics of a wedding day. You are dealing with folks who have heightened emotions. A wedding day can bring out the best or worst in people. Sometimes, unfortunately, I have to be part photographer and part therapist."

*What is the biggest mistake you made early in your career as a wedding photographer? What did you learn from the mistake, and how did you overcome it in the future?*

*McCauley*: "The biggest mistake I made early on in my career was not taking myself seriously from the very beginning. I was an artist who happened to make a business out of her craft. I didn't really put the business aspects into place and pursue real growth until the fourth or fifth year I was in business. That was partly due to fear of the unknown and my own insecurities as a businesswoman. Now, a decade after shooting my first wedding, I find that I am taking more risks. I invest in my education and participate in workshops for myself, and I continuously try to hone my target market since I live in a city with an oversaturated creative industry."

### *What is the biggest misconception up-and-coming photographers have about wedding photography?*

*McCauley*: "That you can charge what veteran wedding photographers charge right out of the gate. I am all for knowing your worth as an artist, but until you have mastered wedding timelines, the dynamics of the day, and have photographed every little detail dozens of times, I think you should price yourself accordingly. That doesn't mean your growth has to be slow. It simply means, put in the work to prove your worth and show you're not a one-wedding wonder!"

### *What are the biggest challenges facing a wedding photographer?*

*McCauley*: "iPhones [smartphones]. I joke, but in all seriousness, it's a huge problem. Not only does everyone think they are a photographer these days, but iPhones have singlehandedly ruined some critical moment images during a wedding day."

### *How has being a wedding photographer changed over the past five years? How have you had to adapt?*

*McCauley*: "Over the past few years, I have found that I am dealing with younger, Millennial clients whose priorities are simply not the same as traditional wedding clients have been in the past. The biggest aspect is promptness. They want all the answers now. I truly believe a potential client would rather get a text message from me with pricing within minutes of sending an inquiry, rather than getting on a phone call, or better yet meeting in person. I've had to adjust how I handle incoming inquiries. The days of sitting down and meeting a couple for coffee have gone out the window."

### *How did you learn to deal with difficult brides and family members while staying professional?*

*McCauley*: "It's all about bringing everything back into perspective for the people involved. I've found that letting people vent and validating that they have been heard is usually the easiest way to move past any difficulties. There are, of course, other occasions where you simply have to keep everyone happy until the day is over and then part ways."

*If someone wants to become a wedding photographer, what is the best way to enter this area of professional photography?*

*McCauley*: "Attend workshops and find a mentor. Shadow, assist, and second shoot as much as possible before venturing out on your own. The guidance from someone who is already doing what you want to be doing is invaluable."

*How important is photographer insurance for wedding photographers?*

*McCauley*: "Insuring yourself as a business is simply a must. Not only are you covering yourself, your gear, and your employees from theft, injury, and damages, for example, but you are also covering any liability that may be held against you. Trust me when I say that people sue businesses over the silliest things, and with the heightened emotions of a wedding, all sorts of scenarios could play out. It's best to be prepared for the worst."

*Since many couples care more about acquiring the digital image files to share online (as opposed to having a photographer create a formal wedding album), what are some of the ways a wedding photographer can still make a good living? Are there add-on services that should be offered?*

*McCauley*: "I have learned to price my collections assuming the couple will not purchase any add-ons. If they do want an album, additional shoot, or other product, that is all a bonus for me. I've found rates that leave me satisfied simply delivering digital files to the couple. As someone who places immense value in the tangible goods of a wedding day, I always encourage a wedding book, but if they choose not to go in that direction, I know I am covered with my original fees."

*What is the best way for a wedding photographer to charge for their services (flat fee, per hour, etc.)? How should they set their rates?*

*McCauley*: "What works best for me might not be the best approach for everyone. I have a flat rate per collection. Each collection has a certain number of hours and other line items included. After that, I have an a la carte menu where add-ons are offered, and upgrades may be selected and purchased. These rates have been set by determining my cost of doing business and my profit goals for my business."

*Based on your experience, what are some of the best ways for a wedding photographer to promote their business and find clients? What works for you and why?*

*McCauley*: "The best way I am able to get new business is by providing an excellent experience to my already existing clients. Positive word of mouth has always been my biggest and most successful form of advertising. It has gotten me the most amount of work."

*What tips do you have for a photographer who needs to create a portfolio to showcase their work?*

*McCauley*: "Attend workshops, and then create stylized shoots to include within your portfolio. Additionally, offer to photograph as much as you can early on so you can build up your body of work. If you are able to, work as a second shooter or as a photographer's assistant for another photographer or company, and ask if you may use those images with proper credit to build your own portoflio. This will all lead to booking gigs that will then replace your styled shoots."

*How important is it for a professional photographer to have an online portfolio/website and to be active on social media?*

*McCauley*: "When recently rebranding my website, I discovered over 60 percent of people are searching and viewing vendors online, many using mobile devices, so having a social media presence and a mobile-friendly website are a must to be considered and taken seriously as a wedding photographer."

*What tips/advance can you offer about branding a wedding photography business (in the real world and online)? How can someone make their business stand out?*

*McCauley*: "Investing in a branding team or designer is a big step. When you can financially do it, you should. It will make all the difference in creating an online presence that is identifiable to your photography. In addition to curating all the pretty [eye-catching content that's well-branded], I highly suggest shooting in a number of different settings and elements as well as photographing different ethnicities. Find where you shine, and really target those areas and clientele."

*Is there any other advice you can offer to people who want to become professional photographers?*

*McCauley*: "While art is subjective, don't fall trap to the comparison game. It's so easy to get caught up in what everyone else is doing. Stay focused, stay driven, take each 'no' with a lesson, and show up for your industry."

## Get Acquainted with Celebrity Photographer Michael Grecco

During his more-than-30-year career as an award-winning professional photographer, Michael Grecco (www.michaelgrecco.com) has served as a photojournalist for the *Associated Press*, *The Boston Herald* newspaper, *People* magazine, and numerous other media organizations. These days, his focus is on celebrity, commercial, and fine art photography. He has been called "the master of light" by his peers and admits to having a fascination with light and its effect in the photographs he takes. "I find magic in its qualities," he says.

Grecco was eager to share his thoughts when asked to be interviewed for this book. He states, "I have no reason to hoard trade secrets. I love sharing knowledge and positive energy. I enjoy fostering the pursuit of creative excellence to fellow photographers." As a Hasselblad Master, he often speaks at conferences, hosts workshops, and teaches photography classes. He's also published several photography books, as his way of giving back to and serving the creative community.

In this interview, Grecco shares his love for photography and delves deeper into what he believes is required to achieve success in this exciting field.

### How did you get into the photography field?

*Grecco*: "I started photography as a kid and was mystified by it. While I was attending Boston University, I got involved with the photojournalism department, although I was registered as a film student. While in school, I got an internship with the Associated Press. Two weeks before the internship was supposed to start, there was a massive blizzard in Boston. I took photos, then skied into the Associated Press office after shooting four rolls of film. Within a few hours, I had my first group of photos on the wire. That was how my career started and what led to my first photos being published.

"I found photojournalism to be fascinating and believed it would provide a great learning experience. As a photojournalist, you're shooting every day. It was a tremendous growing experience as I went from the Associated Press to being a staff photographer at the *Boston Herald*. From the *Boston Herald*, I was invited by *People* magazine to join their staff and move to Los Angeles.

"After moving to Los Angeles, I continued to do photojournalism until I realized that it was no longer my thing. I moved into the more creative portrait realm and focused more on creative, conceptualized, storytelling portraits. I took the skills I learned as a photojournalist and morphed them into magazine photography in a more lyrical, storytelling way that involved a lot more creativity."

*Aside from being a go-getter, what was it that allowed you to move from one awesome job in photography to the next during those early years of your career?*

*Grecco*: "As a photographer, you always have to maintain a good portfolio and work toward improving it. I have always considered myself to be an entrepreneur with multiple businesses and projects going at the same time. If your core business is photography, however, nothing works as well as having great images to showcase. It was always my portfolio that allowed me to get the best jobs.

"In the *People* magazine case, I was shooting the Caroline Kennedy wedding and then the Maria Shriver wedding, and I outshot several of the photographers that *People* magazine had sent to those events. In both cases, *People* magazine wound up picking up images from me. When I was later being considered for a job at *People*, it was those already published images, as opposed to my portfolio, that got their attention and that led to a job offer.

"Magazine photography, and in many other areas and industries that use photographers, the people doing the hiring often use a 'follow the leader' approach to hiring. People will see your work in various places, and then want to hire you based on work they've seen elsewhere. It's sort of a 'proof of concept' approach because it shows you can handle similar assignments and you have the previous work to show it. It allows magazine editors, for example, to reduce their risk and play it safe by hiring photographers who have a proven track record."

*Did you ever have a desire to work with A-list celebrities and have them seek you out to handle their personal and professional photography-related needs?*

*Grecco*: "Not at all. Early on, I wanted to be a portrait photographer. My options were doing corporate portraits, shooting real people, or shooting celebrities where those pictures will get seen over and over again. This is what led to my decision to shoot celebrities. Inherently, the content was appealing to me because I was able to take photos of famous people but use my photography skills to add another layer of importance to those images."

*When you were working as a photojournalist early in your career, the industry was very different than it is today. Would you recommend people pursue photojournalism today?*

*Grecco*: "Today, there is a very small market for photojournalists working in traditional media, and there are already a lot of photographers out there. It's a very difficult market to break into. Newspapers and magazines are constantly downsizing, firing staff, and losing their budgets to hire freelancers. These media outlets are relying on Getty Images and other stock agencies more and more and are paying next to nothing for images.

"At the same time, if you want to be a fashion photographer and work for a fashion magazine, for example, those publishers know they can pay next to nothing for images. If you want to land a job today as a photojournalist working for any type of media organization, it's going to take perseverance and a strong commitment. You've got to be able to take amazing pictures that set you apart. You've got to create something that makes it so people have to have your images. Your images need to become a commodity that people absolutely need and can't live without.

"You also need to be a savvy businessperson to be able to survive as a professional photographer in any field. People want to work with photographers that they get along with, that are easy going on set, but that are able to consistently get the job done. If you're difficult on set or have a bad personality, people won't want to work with you."

*You mentioned it's important for your photography to stand out and a photographer needs to develop their own style. How can an up-and-coming photographer find and then develop their unique style?*

*Grecco*: "Making your work stand out means you have to be willing to take risks. You have to be OK with having a style to begin with and taking the chance that your creative decisions might not work for everyone. You can't expect people to gravitate toward your work if it's ordinary or vanilla. People are always looking for a photographer with an edge or a unique vision. The way to develop your own style is to keep shooting.

"When you're hired to do a shoot, show up really early, set everything up, and start trying different things even before your subject joins you at the shoot. Back in the day, I used to shoot a lot of Polaroids and went into shoots knowing what I liked. I also figured out what worked and didn't work before my subject even arrived at each shoot. Hone your vision before every shoot by trying different things and experimenting, using a stand-in for your subject, if needed.

"On my shoots these days, I always set up a large monitor with a computer attached to it on set and also tether my camera into it. I use that to be able to clearly see what I am doing and then be able to make subtle or dramatic light changes, as needed, for example. By experimenting and making minor aesthetic and creative choices, again even before my subject arrives on set, it helps me to develop my style."

*For a photographer without a big budget, what advice do you have for choosing camera gear?*

*Grecco*: "I believe that the newer camera manufacturers, like Hasselblad, Sony, and Panasonic, have blown away their competition when it comes to the performance of their latest digital SLR and full-frame, mirrorless digital cameras as well as the quality of the optics in their respective lenses. I have shot a *Sports Illustrated* cover, for example, using a Sony camera, as opposed to a Nikon or Canon, which is the gear used by many professionals.

"Right now, whether or not you want to upgrade your camera to a full-frame, mirrorless digital camera is a matter of personal preference. A lot would also be dependent on what you're shooting. The smaller, full-frame, mirrorless cameras are certainly a lot more portable. I am always an advocate of using the right tool for the job at hand."

**What do you think is the biggest misconception up-and-coming photographers have about being a professional photographer?**

*Grecco*: "Many of the photographers trying to enter the industry today have little or no business sense. None understand marketing or how to operate a business. Being a professional photographer requires a lot more than just taking excellent pictures. You've got to learn all aspects of the business, understand how to register copyrights, know how to work with clients in a professional manner, perfect your listening skills, and know how to present yourself. Very few photography schools teach the business side of the photography business, so this knowledge often has to be acquired elsewhere."

**How did you develop your skills working with clients and well-known celebrities?**

*Grecco*: "Patience and good communication are the keys to working with your subjects and clients in a productive way. The first thing I do when I get on a set is sit down with talent, while they're in hair and makeup, for example, and talk to them. I let them know what to expect during the shoot and what's needed from them, and then I listen. You've got to be able to hear and address people's concerns. When it comes to working with difficult people, you need patience and good communication skills.

"Sometimes it's necessary to try what a subject is asking for, even if you're confident that their suggestion won't work. If it does work, you'll be pleasantly surprised, but if it doesn't work, you need to get to a place where you can get what you need. It's important to work with your subject so he or she feels comfortable.

"As the photographer, you have to create a comfortable, stress-free set. I think working with an assistant allows the photographer to focus more on their subject as opposed to the need to tinker with lighting, set pieces, and equipment. The photographer needs to be attentive and connected to the subject. Create an environment that's relaxed. Playing music on set, having food on hand, or offering the subject a glass of wine can make a subject feel more at ease.

"The photographer also needs to be confident and reinforce their subject's confidence. When the subject does something right, compliment them and ask them to do what they just did again. Don't ever get angry or frustrated with your subject. Work with them to get what you need."

### What advice do you have for photographers about setting their rates?

*Grecco*: "Many inexperienced photographers are willing to undermine their own rates and beat the competition's rates in order to land a job. As a result, clients are looking to pay as little as possible. A photographer needs to do their research to figure out what their rates should be and then set rates that are reasonable. I have relationships with other photography friends, and we constantly talk about and compare our rates and offer pricing recommendations to each other.

"Once you get established in your career, having an agent represent you is extremely useful. They know the market and can help you set your rates, while helping with client relations, for example."

### What are some of the ways that you market and promote your photography business?

*Grecco*: "I do a little bit of everything. For example, I regularly do email campaigns, and I am active on social media. I also use portfolio showings, direct mail, and networking to generate new business. Also, I have a well-designed website. At this point, I have someone working for me who handles search engine optimization for my website as well as someone who handles Facebook and Google Ads advertising. I also work with a public relations agency that sends out press releases and another that focuses on getting me featured in the media and who sets up interviews. It's become a relatively complex system that comes together to build visibility for my work. In terms of other employees, I now have a full-time studio manager, archivist, and a researcher on my staff."

### What tips can you offer when it comes to branding a photography business?

*Grecco*: "Having a professional-looking logo is important. When you're working in many areas of photography, you'll need to deal with creative people. If you show that you can put together a website that looks good and functions well, aside from the photography work itself, it shows that you have taste, and that's important. If your website looks amateurish or just awful, but your photography looks great, that's detrimental to the photography and reflects poorly on you as the photographer.

"Having a logo, website, business cards, letterhead, and social media content that's well-designed all works toward building a respectable brand. All these tools should stick to the brand you've created and offer continuity and consistency."

*Is there any additional advice you'd like to offer to up-and-coming photographers?*

*Grecco*: "Yes. Don't give up! Persistence is what this business is all about. You need to keep believing in yourself and in your work."

## Learn More About Wedding and Event Photography from Rob Grant

In his own right, Rob Grant is a highly successful wedding photographer, who is hired to shoot more than 50 weddings per year. His full-time job, however, is as a photo specialist for Nations Photo Lab (www.nationsphotolab.com).

Mentioned several times throughout this book as being an excellent resource for pro photographers, Nations Photo Lab is a full-service photography lab that's based in Hunt Valley, Maryland. Grant explains, "Our company's products are made by photographers, with photographers in mind—from professional-quality photo prints to handcrafted wall decor. We believe your precious moments deserve more than to remain forgotten as files on your phone or laptop. They deserve to live on in print for years to come.

"Our high-quality photo prints are our specialty. We offer more than 60 sizes on three different paper types, including Kodak Endura Premier Lustre, Kodak Endura Premier Metallic, and Kodak Endura Premier Glossy. While our professional quality is similar to other big labs, our prices are lower," adds Grant. "We know that life gets busy for professional photographers, which is why we offer a partnership with ImageQuix. This service provides professional studios with a complete online proofing and ordering system. You shoot, you post, your customers order, and Nations Photo Lab prints and ships. It's the most profitable solution for selling your photos online."

As you will discover by visiting Nations Photo Lab's website, the company offers many solutions for helping pro photographers increase their revenue. They have a broad selection of top-quality prints and photo products for pro photographers to offer to their customers and clients.

"We've created numerous products with the professional photographer in mind," Grant explains. "Our Album99 features handcrafted covers, flush mounted pages, and heirloom-quality construction. Its pricing starts at $99, giving pros less business overhead. We also offer bulk discounts on our bestselling print sizes. Plus, we know how important branding is to a successful photography business, so we offer custom imprinted USB [flash] drives for delivering photos to your clients, as well as unique packaging for your flash drives and prints."

Every business day, Grant interacts with pro photographers from around the world through his work with Nations Photo Lab. On weekends, he typically works as a wedding photographer and experiences firsthand the trials and tribulations of earning a living as a photographer. In this interview, Grant offers some excellent advice to up-and-coming wedding photographers, but much of this advice also applies to shooting any type of events.

*What made you want to become a wedding photographer?*

*Grant*: "I have been involved with many styles of photography over the years. One of my favorite things about weddings is that they incorporate all those styles. On a typical wedding day, I will shoot portraits, candid photojournalistic images, macro closeup detail shots, architectural and/or landscape images, and capture split-second moments of action, using techniques similar to what would be used in sports photography. For this reason, I find weddings very interesting and challenging to shoot, which is what encouraged me to pursue the craft professionally."

*What photography education/experience/training did you have?*

*Grant*: "I was initially self-taught and was hired to assist and second shoot for one of the best wedding photographers in my hometown. My photography-related education came mostly from on-the-job training. Practice sessions and photo critiques from pros helped me develop and improve my skills. Eventually I was doing jobs as a lead photographer and ultimately moved on to my own business. Nowadays, there is a ton of online training available, plus workshops and trade shows, where someone can obtain a more formal education."

*Beyond being able to take pictures, what additional skills are needed to become a good wedding photographer?*

*Grant*: "Business knowledge, good people skills to deal with a wide variety of personality types, a lot of patience, and the ability to stay calm and execute perfectly under pressure."

*What is the biggest drawback and best perk of being a wedding photographer?*

*Grant*: "I think it often comes as a surprise to new photographers that many hours of work are involved, both before and after shooting a wedding. This can definitely be a drawback, and it's important to find a balance between personal time and work. There are many perks, however. The pay is good. Generally, weddings are a very happy occasion, taking place in beautiful locations, and there's often good food. More important, you know you are creating priceless photos that will be in the wedding couple's family forever."

*What is the biggest mistake you made early on in your career as a wedding photographer? What did you learn from the mistake, and how did you overcome it in the future?*

*Grant*: "I started shooting with film and then switched to digital. I was slow to properly learn Adobe Photoshop and Adobe Lightroom. As a result, I wasted a lot of time doing post-production work after each wedding. I have since honed my skills so I can process digital images quickly and effectively. This is critical since you will be processing thousands of images per week. Some photographers outsource their image editing, but I prefer to keep that in my own hands."

*What is the biggest misconception up-and-coming photographers have about wedding photography?*

*Grant*: "I think many photographers don't realize the wide range of shooting situations they will face and are not technically prepared for what's in store for them. It's also a shock to many photographers to learn how much equipment is needed to properly do the job. I strongly recommend always having backup equipment on hand because things will go wrong."

*What are the biggest challenges facing a wedding photographer?*

*Grant*: "You only have one chance to get it right, and the locations, shooting conditions, shooting techniques, and your equipment needs can change drastically from wedding to wedding. You might have an easy wedding one week, with cooperative clients, beautiful natural light, and plenty of time. This would cause you to think that wedding photography is pretty easy. But then during the next wedding, everything can change and be much more difficult. You might encounter uncooperative or late clients, a rushed time schedule, very difficult lighting situations, and/or very restrictive church rules. As a pro, you need to learn how to deliver professional caliber images in all situations."

*How has being a wedding photographer changed over the past five years? How have you had to adapt?*

*Grant*: "There are tons of new photographers going into business all the time. The competition for each job is often intense. It's important to continue to learn and grow as a photographer and to always give 100 percent effort to achieve top quality images at each wedding. Always trying out new ideas and shooting techniques will help you to stand out and also keep you creatively motivated."

*How did you learn to deal with difficult brides and family members while staying professional?*

*Grant*: "It helps if you have a naturally calm demeanor and are able to perform well under pressure. These abilities will continue to improve with practice when you experience 'real wedding pressure' firsthand. It also helps to get your feet wet dealing with this stress as a second photographer [shooter] before starting to do your own jobs as the lead."

***If someone wants to become a wedding photographer, what is the best way to enter this area of professional photography?***

*Grant*: "I think the best way is to assist and second shoot for an established photographer. That way, you can watch a seasoned pro and see how they handle all the challenges of a wedding day. Plus, you can start building up your portfolio without the pressure of being the lead photographer."

***What are the most essential pieces of photography equipment a wedding photographer must have?***

*Grant*: "First of all you need to have at least two of everything in case of equipment failure. That means a minimum of two cameras, two flashes, and multiple lenses covering from 24-200mm. You'll often need the wide lens for ceremony shots to show the whole scene and all the guests, particularly in a large, beautiful church. Sometimes the church rules will force you to stand all the way in the back or perhaps shoot from the balcony, so you'll need a long telephoto lens for that.

"I prefer zoom lenses and to use a 24mm to 70mm and/or 24mm to 120mm, plus an 80mm to 200mm. I also bring a 14mm to 24mm and a 105mm macro lens for detail shots of the rings. I use radio triggers to control my flashes for off-camera flash work. Many photographers primarily shoot with 35mm and 85mm prime lenses with a 1.4 or 1.8 aperture. That is a popular option that has the advantage of a very shallow depth of field. But the downside is that you have to move to change your composition closer or farther, and often your movement is limited by church rules, tables, and wedding guests. For this reason, I prefer to use zoom lenses. I actually bring three cameras, four flashes, and six lenses to most weddings."

***How important is photographer insurance for wedding photographers?***

*Grant*: "It's very important for photographers to have both equipment and liability insurance to protect their equipment in case of theft and yourself in case of an accident that could result in a lawsuit. Also, some venues will insist that you have liability insurance or you can't work on their property."

*Since many couples care more about acquiring the digital image files to share online (as opposed to having a photographer create a wedding album), what are some of the ways a wedding photographer can still make a good living? Are there add-on services that should be offered?*

*Grant*: "Set your day rate so that you will make an acceptable profit from just the digital files. Selling products on top of that will increase your revenue and profit potential. Some photographers don't offer products, others offer products a la carte, and some photographers insist on an album being included in every package. If you offer products, do in-home sales sessions or create an online image gallery where people can view and order prints or products."

### What is the best way for a wedding photographer to charge for their services?

*Grant*: "The prices charged will vary greatly depending on your local market. A photographer in New York City will typically charge more than someone in a small town in the Midwest. I only shoot one wedding per day and typically prefer a flat rate for the entire day. Other photographers have had success charging per hour and focus more on shooting shorter weddings. For instance, it's common for some beach weddings to be very quick, so some photographers will shoot several in a day."

### Do you have a personalized wedding photography shot list that you typically work from?

*Grant*: "I try to avoid working from a shot list because I want to be able to react to what's uniquely happening at that particular wedding instead of a cliched list that a bride saw in a magazine. Many of the standard shots are things that any pro already knows to shoot, such as the bride with their bridesmaids and the groom with their groomsmen, so I don't need that on a list.

"I do pay close attention to the requested family combinations because that can vary quite a bit from one wedding to another. I always ask if there is anything unusual happening that I need to be aware of, such as a special shot with college friends or an organized sparkler exit at the end of the night."

### Based on your experience, what are some of the best ways for a wedding photographer to promote their business and find clients? What works for you and why?

*Grant*: "Referrals from former clients and other wedding vendors are the best because they have actually worked with you, so it's a personal recommendation. Paying for advertising often has mixed results, and it can get expensive. Be sure to ask every person who inquires about your services how they heard about you."

*What tips do you have for a photographer who needs to create a portfolio to showcase their best work?*

*Grant*: "Ideally, work with another photographer to gain experience as you build your portfolio. You can also advertise to do some free or low-cost nonwedding day photo shoots as a low-stress way to learn and get more images for your portfolio.

"There are also workshops with models in wedding dresses that you can participate in. Finally, if you attend a wedding as a guest, bring your camera and try to get some images, but always make sure you don't get in the way of the hired pro. Watch how the pro works and introduce yourself during a lull in the action. Maybe get some free tips. Plus, you can use that as an opportunity to see if the pro is looking for an intern, assistant, or second shooter."

*How important is it for a professional photographer to have an online portfolio/website and to be active on social media?*

*Grant*: "It's critical to have an online presence. A nice clean website that's easy to navigate, along with social media posts related to your recent jobs will be very helpful in getting new clients. Only show your best work. Less is more. Most people won't look through hundreds of images, so always showcase your best work first."

*Is there any other advice you can offer to people who want to become professional photographers?*

*Grant*: "Learn your craft before committing yourself to covering a wedding as the only photographer. Again, start as an assistant or second photographer, practice nonwedding day photo shoots, have a pro critique your images, and make sure you have decent equipment with backups before you accept a real wedding assignment. Remember it's an event that can't be rescheduled, so you have to respect that and show up fully prepared."

## Photographers Daniel and Laura Pinckard Share Their Wisdom

Husband-and-wife team Daniel and Laura Pinckard operate their own wedding photography business, called Laura Pinckard, LLC (www.laurapinckard.com). "Before becoming wedding photographers, we were photography enthusiasts, mostly focused on portraits. Ultimately, we decided to enter the wedding industry because it offered an opportunity to take our passion for photography and make it more meaningful. When we got married, we were very disappointed with our own wedding photos. We received much fewer than expected, many were out of focus, and they didn't look very professional. As wedding photographers, we can almost make up for our own disappointment by ensuring that other couples are in love with their wedding photos," explains Laura.

Both Daniel and Laura are self-taught photographers. They have relied heavily on instructional YouTube videos and articles to obtain their knowledge. Daniel adds, "Before becoming full-time wedding photographers, we did have some experience second shooting as well as taking photos of elopement ceremonies."

*In the next two to three years, do you believe it will be necessary for all professional photographers to upgrade to full-frame, mirrorless digital cameras?*

*Laura*: "Not necessarily within two to three years, but it will most likely be necessary to upgrade to mirrorless cameras at some point. As camera manufacturers produce new models over the next few years, I expect the mirrorless camera specs and features to significantly surpass those that DSLRs can offer. Eventually, the difference will be too great to continue using DSLRs professionally."

*Beyond being able to take pictures, what additional skills are needed to become a good photographer?*

*Daniel*: "To be successful as a wedding photographer, you need to do three things. First, you have to take good photos. Second, you need to provide a good customer experience to every single client. This requires good people skills and organizational skills. Lastly, you must be able to book new clients, which involves good marketing and sales skills."

*What is the biggest drawback and best perk of being a wedding photographer?*

*Laura*: "The biggest drawback is all the work and planning that takes place in the background. Taking photos of the wedding is a blast, but there is so much work that many prospective photographers don't even think about that takes a significant amount of time.

"The best perk of being a wedding photographer is the excitement and joy that you get to be a part of. Weddings are a lot of fun to shoot. It's about sharing a special, intimate moment with the couple and their closest friends and family. Being the person who captures those moments makes you instantly become a significant part of that couple's lives. Another perk is that wedding photography is one of the highest paying photography gigs that you can get, as long as you market to the right clients."

*What is the biggest misconception up-and-coming photographers have about wedding photography?*

*Daniel*: "The biggest misconception is that it is an easy way to make a quick buck. Many photographers hear how much wedding photographers charge and say, 'Wow, I should get into that industry.' In reality, we sometimes make more per hour doing engagement and portrait shoots than we do at weddings. There are so many additional hours beyond just the wedding day that reduce your return on investment, so it's not a way to get rich quick."

### What are the biggest challenges facing a wedding photographer?

*Laura*: "One of the biggest challenges is actually booking clients. The wedding industry is full of couples who are price shopping because planning a wedding is extremely expensive. Oftentimes, those couples will contact a dozen or more different photographers but only respond back to one or two, leaving the other group wondering if the couple received their email or if they said something wrong.

"In our experience, making a personal connection right off the bat is the best way to go. If you can add something personal, even 'stalking' [following] the perspective client on social media, your chances of hearing back from the couple go up tenfold."

### How has being a wedding photographer changed over the past five years? How have you had to adapt?

*Daniel*: "As DSLR cameras have become more affordable, many photography enthusiasts have begun calling themselves wedding photographers without fully committing to it full time. Those wedding photographers charge significantly less because it is not their full-time income, which has been a cause of frustration for many professional photographers.

"The best way to deal with this challenge is to communicate a value proposition that those part-time photographers can't offer. For us, the unique value that we offer is our specific style of photography. It differs from traditional, posed photos. We pride ourselves in consistent editing, and couples see that in our portfolio. Once prospective clients fall in love with our unique shooting style, it really doesn't matter how much we charge."

### How did you learn to deal with difficult brides and family members while staying professional?

*Laura*: "Dealing with difficult clients is not unique to wedding photography. It's just the nature of a customer-centric business. To succeed in any business, you need to provide a positive customer experience, despite how frustrating it may be for you.

"It really helps to remember that the bride is experiencing one of the most important days of her life, and she has dreamed about it for years. We try to be as flexible as possible and never express any of our own frustrations during the wedding day because honestly, that would be extremely selfish and unprofessional."

***If someone wants to become a wedding photographer, what's the best way to enter this area of professional photography?***

*Daniel*: "Wedding photography is a delicate industry. If you make a mistake, you can't get a do-over. Before becoming a full-time professional wedding photographer, you need to get experience and build up a strong portfolio.

"You can do this by associate shooting with other photographers, attending styled photo shoots and workshops, and offering significant discounts to your first few clients. When we got married, our wedding photographer let us believe that he had plenty of experience, when in reality, he had only worked as a second shooter for a couple weddings. We were obviously very disappointed with the result and would never recommend him, even though he might have plenty of experience now."

***What are the most essential pieces of photography equipment a wedding photographer must have?***

*Laura*: "Wedding photographers should be prepared for anything. We bring extra camera bodies, multiple lenses, on-camera flashes, external lighting equipment, tripods, and plenty of batteries and SD cards. You never know if something is going to break or if poor weather will force you to take portraits inside a dark building.

"We also keep two SD cards in each of our cameras and use the second one to back up the files because the worst thing that can happen is losing all of the photos."

***How important is photographer insurance for wedding photographers?***

*Daniel*: "Insurance is very important for multiple reasons. First, you can never plan for things that might go wrong. Insurance can protect you in worst-case scenarios. Additionally, many venues require the wedding vendors to be insured. Without proper insurance, you will likely miss out on photography gigs that you would have otherwise booked."

***Since many couples care more about acquiring the digital image files to share online (as opposed to having a photographer create a wedding album), what are some of the ways a wedding photographer can still make a good living? Are there add-on services that should be offered?***

*Laura*: "We primarily just offer online galleries with high resolution downloads because that's what couples are looking for. Ultimately, booking more clients is better than selling add-ons to a few clients. We keep our packages clean and simple, and it makes it so much easier to book with us. Some clients will still inquire about albums or prints, but we don't push it. A great add-on suggestion is engagement photos that can be used for save-the-dates."

### What is the best way for a wedding photographer to charge for their services?

*Daniel*: "Most couples are expecting a flat fee for a photography package. This pricing structure keeps it simple and upfront so there is no confusion later. When some photographers charge per hour or bill their clients for hotel, food, and gas receipts, the cost can get significantly higher than expected, resulting in unhappy clients. While the photographer might make more money initially, it is more profitable to get positive reviews and referrals from past clients. A deceptive pricing structure will do the opposite."

### Based on your experience, what are some of the best ways for a wedding photographer to promote their business and find clients?

*Laura*: "This depends slightly on the photographer's target market. Ours is young couples who are looking for candid, intimate photos, so Instagram is one of our most useful marketing tools. For photographers who are targeting higher-end clients, it would make more sense to invest in exhibitions at wedding shows. Each photographer should determine who their target audience is and where those prospective clients spend most of their time. With that in mind, content marketing can be extremely useful.

"We are also based in a region with little competition, so website search engine optimization [SEO] is very cost effective. In Google's local search results, we are the number-one result for many queries, which drives a lot of traffic to our website."

### What tips do you have for a photographer who needs to create a portfolio to showcase their best work?

*Daniel*: "To build your portfolio, you should attend styled shoots that fit the style that will attract your target market. Many photographers and wedding planners work together to create styled shoots, and they put a lot of effort into the design. Having those high-quality photos in your portfolio, on your website, on business cards, and displayed within your marketing materials, will make a tremendous impact."

### How important is it for a professional photographer to have an online portfolio/website and to be active on social media?

*Laura*: "For our target audience, it is very important. Without a social media presence, most of our couples would never have found us. Our website makes the booking process very easy.

"At the same time, many photographers can be extremely successful through networking and by attending wedding shows. It ultimately comes down to finding out where your specific target market spends their time and then focusing the majority of your attention in those areas.

"Conducting brief and informal surveys with your past clients can be very helpful. Did most of them find you through recommendations from other wedding professionals? If so, how can you take your relationships with those professionals to a new level through bundle packages or cross-promotions?"

### What tips/advance can you offer about branding a photography business (in the real world and online)?

*Daniel*: "Branding is something that we feel strongly about. In order to succeed, you can't just be a generic 'wedding photographer.' You need to offer some sort of unique value, and your brand needs to be known for that value.

"We focus on adventurous, outdoor photos with mountainous backdrops. If you look at our website and social media, you will consistently see intimate couple photos, and the subjects are surrounded by beautiful outdoor scenery. Couples hire us because that's the style that they're looking for, and they often drive hours out of their way, past dozens of other photographers, for an hour-long photo shoot with us.

"The same goes for wedding clients. If a couple is planning a wedding with a very specific style of decorations, colors, and location, they will look for a photographer whose brand fits that style. For effective branding, you should use consistent phrasing to describe your business, display photos with a consistent style, and use the same color scheme and design elements for your website and anything else that you use for marketing. Consistency is extremely important."

### Is there any other advice you can offer to people who want to become professional wedding photographers?

*Laura*: "Stay positive about everything. It will make you happier and more successful. Many photographers complain about clients on their social media, talk badly about other photographers, or talk about how much they hate editing photos.

"When potential clients hear negativity, it doesn't build trust. In fact, it does the opposite. Likewise, when other wedding professionals hear it, they most likely will avoid recommending you to their clients. I am very selective about the other professionals in my industry who I am willing to recommend, and I specifically avoid recommending anyone who gossips or complains. If my clients have a bad experience with that person, that automatically looks bad for me."

## Photographer Mark Campbell Offers Some Words of Wisdom

Located in Chicago, Mark Campbell (www.markcampbellphotography.com) is an internationally recognized, award-winning commercial photographer and videographer. He founded his company, MCP (Mark Campbell Productions), in 2010.

He is a sought-after photographer and works with many corporate clients and magazines. Some of his clients include Fortune 500 companies and many marketing and advertising agencies, as well as Ameritrade, The Art Institute of Chicago, Heineken, Microsoft, Northwestern University, Oracle, and Warby Parker eyewear. He is regularly called on to shoot corporate headshots, corporate events, and branding-related images for his clients.

In addition to running his company from a business standpoint, he serves as its creative director.

*Beyond being able to take great photos, what are the core skills a professional photographer needs to have to be successful?*

*Campbell*: "Beyond creating great photos, a successful photographer needs to have good interpersonal skills, be well organized, and have strong computer skills."

*What are some of your tips for succeeding as a pro photographer?*

*Campbell*: "One of my biggest tips for up-and-coming photographers is to always arrive early to a shoot and be fully prepared. Ensure that your camera batteries are fully charged and you have plenty of storage space available within your memory cards.

"It's also important for you, as the photographer, to be well-dressed and nicely groomed. This is especially necessary if you're working with corporate clients and executives at advertising or marketing agencies, for example.

"I also believe it's necessary to be responsive across all forms of communication. Use your client's preferred communication method, and always respond to them promptly. Then, when discussing a project, as the photographer, it's your responsibility to manage expectations and all deliverables. Finally, protect your data! Maintain reliable backups in multiple locations."

*What are some of the best ways for photographers to brand and then promote their business?*

*Campbell*: "It is critical for photographers to have brand identity, then create a website that represents that brand with a consistent look and feel before extending that presence to social channels. Having quality business cards and at least one other print marketing piece that you can leave behind for grassroots marketing efforts is equally important. After the brand and marketing executions are in place, consider advertising on Yelp, Google, or an industry-specific platform similar to The Knot."

*What are some of your best tips for compiling and showcasing a portfolio?*

*Campbell*: "Your portfolio should contain between 25 and 30 images. They should all be from different jobs/shoots and specific to one category. For example, a 'headshots portfolio' should only contain headshots and not event photos. As you get started, be prepared to shoot things for a discounted rate or for free to build your portfolio."

*What is the biggest misconception people have about what it takes to be a successful pro photographer?*

*Campbell*: "People often overlook all of the nonphoto-taking elements of a photography business, including the office management and client management sides. There is also the 'I am going to be a fashion model photographer right out of the gate' mentality. Younger photographers can suffer from this and do not want to shoot 'less cool' jobs in order to build their business and establish themselves in the industry."

*When it comes to buying a camera and gear, what are your best tips?*

*Campbell*: "When buying gear, it is best to choose your brand, such as Canon, Sony, or Nikon, early and then invest in that brand. Lenses will have a longer shelf life in the course of a career, making it a safer place to invest. Camera technologies are changing quickly, so it can be helpful to own lenses and rent cameras."

# Resources

They say you can never be rich enough or thin enough. While that's arguable, we firmly believe you can never have enough resources. Therefore, we're giving you a wealth of sources to check into, check out, and harness for your own personal information blitz.

These sources are tidbits—ideas to get you started on your research. They are by no means the only sources out there, and they should not be taken as the ultimate answer. We have done our research, but businesses tend to move, change, fold, and expand. As we have repeatedly stressed, do your homework. Get out there and start investigating!

## Photography Associations

American Photographic Artists: https://apanational.org/events/upcoming

American Society of Media Photographers: www.asmp.org

American Society of Picture Professionals: http://aspp.com

National Press Photographers Association: https://nppa.org

Professional Photographers of America: www.ppa.com

Professional Women Photographers: www.pwponline.org

Society of International Fashion & Glamour Photographers: www.sifgp.com

Special Kids Photography of America: www.specialkidsphotography.com

Wedding & Portrait Photography International: www.wppiexpo.com

Wedding Photojournalist Association: www.wpja.com

Women in Photography International: www.womeninphotography.org

## Photography Franchise Resources

Entrepreneur: www.entrepreneur.com/franchises/category/svcphoto

Franchise Direct: www.franchisedirect.com

Franchise Rankings:
www.franchiserankings.com/reviews-and-ratings-of-best-photography-franchises

## Photo Product Sales Sites

CafePress: www.cafepress.com

Redbubble: www.redbubble.com

Vistaprint: www.vistaprint.com

Zazzle: www.zazzle.com

## Web and Portfolio Design

Jimdo: www.jimdo.com

PhotoDeck: www.photodeck.com

ShootProof: www.shootproof.com

SmugMug: www.smugmug.com

Squarespace: www.squarespace.com/tour/photography-websites

Weebly: www.weebly.com/photography-websites

Wix: www.wix.com/html5us/photographer

WordPress: https://wordpress.org

Zenfolio: https://zenfolio.com

## *Products and Services for Professionals*

AdoramaPix: www.adoramapix.com/metal-prints-sem

Backdrop Express: www.backdropexpress.com

Backdrop Outlet: www.backdropoutlet.com

Bay Photo Lab: www.bayphoto.com/wall-displays/metalprints

Denny Manufacturing: www.dennymfg.com

Full Color: www.fullcolor.com

Mpix: www.mpix.com/products/modern-metal-prints

Nations Photo Lab: www.nationsphotolab.com

NextDayFliers: www.nextdayflyers.com/banner-printing/backdrops.php

Photo Pie Backdrops: www.photopiebackdrops.com/Photography-Backdrops

PortraitPro: www.portraitprofessional.com

SmugMug: www.smugmug.com

## *Camera Equipment and Rentals*

Adorama: www.adorama.com

B&H Photo Video: www.bhphotovideo.com

BorrowLenses.com: www.borrowlenses.com

CameraLens Rentals: www.cameralensrentals.com

Lensrentals: www.lensrentals.com

## Stock Agencies

Getty Images: www.gettyimages.com

iStock: www.istockphoto.com

## Education and Training

Adobe Certification Training: www.adobe.com/training/certification.html

Coursera: www.coursera.org

edX: www.edx.org

iTunes U: https://itunes.apple.com/us/app/itunes-u/id490217893

New York Institute of Photography: www.nyip.com

Udemy: www.udemy.com

## Scholarships

Coca-Cola Scholars Foundation: www.coca-colascholarsfoundation.org

CollegeXpress: www.collegexpress.com

College Scholarships: www.college-scholarships.com

Fastweb: www.fastweb.com

Scholarships.com: www.scholarships.com

SuperCollege.com: www.supercollege.com

## General Business Planning Software

LivePlan: www.liveplan.com

Business Plan Pro: www.businessplanpro.com

Growthink: https://strategicplantemplate.growthink.com

# Glossary

**All rights**: the unrestricted right to reproduce, distribute, display, and publish an image; not a copyright transfer

**Assignment**: agreement to produce photographic images according to client specifications, to be used only in the manner described by a grant of usage rights

**Background**: area shown behind the main subject in a picture

**Bid**: legally binding proposal formulated by a photographer based on the scope of a project description

**Candid pictures**: images where the subject does not pose; often taken without the subject's knowledge

**Copyright**: given to the legal owner of a photograph or piece of work

**Copyright infringement**: act of violating a copyright owner's exclusive rights

**Day rate**: pre-agreed, flat-rate fee paid for up to one day of production work

**DSLR**: digital single-lens reflex camera that allows the photographer to look through the lens and see exactly what image will be captured

**Embargo period**: a period of time during which an image may not be licensed, published, and/or distributed

**Estimate**: an approximation of fees and costs formulated by photographer based on the scope of the project description, nonbinding

**Flash**: brief, bright illumination caused by an artificial light source

**Full-Frame Mirrorless Digital Camera**: a new generation of digital cameras that offer interchangeable lenses, but do not use a mirror to reflect the image into the camera's viewfinder like a Digital SLR camera

**Gray market**: these are products manufactured by a specific company that are being sold in countries they were not meant to be sold in. When it comes to digital cameras, gray market Canon SLR cameras being sold in the U.S., for example, are manufactured by Canon, but not intended for sale within the U.S. Both versions of the camera model may be the same, but the gray market version of the camera will likely be very different.

**Image**: a likeness of a real object or person, produced electronically, through a lens, or in a picture

**Lens**: optical device made of glass or plastic and capable of bending and focusing light

**Metadata**: this is information about a digital image, such as the time, date, and location it was taken, that gets stored with the image's digital file. Metadata can also include the camera settings used to take a photo, or a text-based caption added to the file by the photographer.

**Photo Product**: this is a custom-designed product, such as a T-shirt, coffee mug, mouse pad, puzzle, calendar, or poster size print that's designed using a specific digital photograph

**Print**: a photographic image on paper

**Shutter**: camera device that controls the duration of the exposure by opening and closing the lens aperture

**Still life**: inanimate subject arranged to make full use of form, shape, and lighting

**Stock photography**: images being sold, licensed, or made available from a stock photo agency that is typically sold or licensed on a non-exclusive basis

**Subject**: the person or thing being photographed, which is the primary focal point of the image

**Tripod**: three-legged camera support that can usually be height-adjusted

# Index